SECURING
your FUTURE

SECURING *your* FUTURE

OLADAPO OLARINMOYE

XULON PRESS

Xulon Press
2301 Lucien Way #415
Maitland, FL 32751
407.339.4217
www.xulonpress.com

© 2020 by Oladapo Olarinmoye

All rights reserved solely by the author. The author guarantees all contents are original and do not infringe upon the legal rights of any other person or work. No part of this book may be reproduced in any form without the permission of the author. The views expressed in this book are not necessarily those of the publisher.

Unless otherwise indicated, Scripture quotations taken from the King James Version (KJV)–*public domain.*

Paperback ISBN-13: 978-1-6322-1901-5

Ebook ISBN-13: 978-1-6322-1902-2

Dedication

I dedicate this book to my parents Joseph Olajide and Victoria Ebunoluwa Olarinmoye who laboured tirelessly over the years to prepare and secure a future for my siblings and I. May their gentle souls rest in peace.

Table of Contents

Dedication...v
Acknowledgments..ix
Introduction..xi

Chapter One
Securing Your Finances with God........................... 1

Chapter Two
Following The Right Path To Success 9

Chapter Three
Making Godly Decisions................................... 23

Chapter Four
Adopting The Right Attitude For Your Success 31

Chapter Five
Discovering Your Buried Potentials....................... 45

Chapter Six
Discovering The Resources Around You 59

Chapter Seven
Choosing To Be Rich 69

Chapter Eight
Deploying Your God Given Skills.......................... 77

Chapter Nine
Harnessing The Possibilities Of The Mind 87

SECURING YOUR FUTURE

Chapter Ten
Dealing With The Limitations In Your Mind................95

Chapter Eleven
Mapping Out Plans Of Action............................101

Chapter Twelve
Receiving Answers From God 111

Last Words And Prayers.................................119
References..123

Acknowledgments

I wish to first and foremost thank my Heavenly Father, The Almighty God for depositing in me the inspiration and insights to write this book. May His name be forever glorified.

I wish to thank members of RCCG Salvation Centre where I had the opportunity to first share some of the insights in this book. In particular I wish to appreciate Brother Oluwanifishe Taiwo, Sister Odunsi and Sister Yinka Alawode for their professionalism and persistence in getting me to birth this book. I wish to thank members of RCCG Graceland who are presently giving me a platform to practice and preach the insights in this book.

I thank my brother Wole Olarinmoye and my sisters, Kemi Oluwagbemi, Lola Awobowale and Bukola Ojo for offering their suggestions to improve the quality of this book.

I specially thank my daughter Mofopefoluwa for proof reading and editing the manuscript.

I thank both my daughter Mofopefoluwa and my son Moboluwarin for believing in me and for encouraging me to be a better version of myself.

SECURING YOUR FUTURE

Finally, I must thank my dear wife, Abayomi for her love, support, encouragement and worthwhile contributions towards getting this book ready and printed.

May the Lord bless you all richly in Jesus Name, for making this book a reality, Thank you.

Introduction

Wouldn't you love to be fully assured that your future is secured no matter what happens on the earth? The things that are now happening on the earth are indications that the systems that people trust in are not certain.

For example, the year 2009 brought major financial challenges worldwide that is still influencing companies, families, and individuals alike. Many companies were forced to close, many others had to downsize. Many homeowners lost their homes, as they could no longer afford their mortgage payments. Many families had to drastically change their lifestyle, as their monthly income was no longer enough or no longer available to meet their needs. Many individuals became perpetual debtors, as they could no longer pay their debts and just could not balance their inflows and outflows. For all these people, the world system had failed them.

The year 2020 brought upon us a pandemic, the coronavirus (COVID-19), which made the entire world to essentially shut down for a few months. The world powers had no answer and were subject to the same problem as smaller, lesser developed countries.

Airlines, hotels, businesses, schools, churches, and marketplaces were shut down to help contain the spread of the virus and to reduce the fatalities. There were travel restrictions leading planes to be grounded and airports were shut down. Several businesses could no longer earn revenue and had to declare bankruptcy, many employees lost their jobs, others received a reduction in their income, and many found it difficult to pay their rents and many found it difficult to afford food to eat. Once again, the world system had failed them.

Some rich people have suddenly become debtors. The world system that had previously protected them and made them rich has failed.

However, there is a system that neither changes nor fails. This system is governed by the principles laid out in the Word of God. It is known as God's system. God's system is able to withstand all kinds of global meltdowns, whether financial, health-related, or natural disasters.

In Matthew 6:19-20 the Bible states,

"Lay not up for yourselves treasures upon earth, where moth and rust doth corrupt, and where thieves break through and steal: But lay up for yourselves treasures in heaven, where neither moth nor rust doth corrupt, and where thieves do not break through nor steal:" (Matthew 6:19-20, KJV)

There is nothing that you lay up for yourself that cannot be destroyed. It can be affected by fire, ill-health, death, armed robbers, pandemics, etc.

The Bible encourages you to lay up for yourselves treasures in Heaven because the world system has no influence over God's system. God's system does not fail. It is secure against fire, ill health, pandemics etc.

In Psalms 37:18-19 the Bible states,

INTRODUCTION

"The LORD knoweth the days of the upright: and their inheritance shall be for ever. They shall not be ashamed in the evil time: and in the days of famine they shall be satisfied." (Psalms 37:18-19, KJV)

The Lord has the answers and He knows what needs to be done to keep lack and famine far away from your home. He will keep destruction and shame away and satisfy all your needs in Jesus' name.

I once heard the story of someone who secured his house with several high-pitch alarms. He was on his bed when the armed robbers came to knock on his bedroom door. They had blasted into the house through the wall. The alarms and gadgets were not sufficient to prevent the robbers from gaining entrance into his house.

In Psalm 127 verse 1, the Bible states that

"Except the LORD build the house, they labour in vain that build it: except the LORD keep the city, the watchman waketh but in vain." (Psalms 127:1, KJV)

The Lord is the one who can build and secure our lives, homes, and future for us.

In Proverbs 13 verse 22, the Bible states that

"A good man leaveth an inheritance to his children's children: and the wealth of the sinner is laid up for the just." (Proverbs 13:22, KJV)

My desire is that as you read this book you will learn from the Lord how to secure not just your own future, but also the future of your children and the future of your children's children in the name of Jesus.

Chapter One

Securing Your Finances with God

Only God can help you to secure your future and the future of your children. A good example of a man that God helped to secure the future of his children after his death was one of Elisha's aides. This can be found in 2 Kings 4: 1- 7

"Now there cried a certain woman of the wives of the sons of the prophets unto Elisha, saying, Thy servant my husband is dead; and thou knowest that thy servant did fear the LORD: and the creditor is come to take unto him my two sons to be bondmen. And Elisha said unto her, what shall I do for thee? tell me, what hast thou in the house? And she said, thine handmaid hath not anything in the house, save a pot of oil. Then he said, Go, borrow thee vessels abroad of all thy neighbours, even empty vessels; borrow not a few. And when thou art come in, thou shalt shut the door upon thee and upon thy sons, and shalt pour out into all those vessels, and thou shalt set aside that which is full. So, she went from him, and shut the door upon her and upon her sons, who brought the vessels to her; and she poured out. And it came to pass, when the vessels were full, that she said unto her son, Bring me yet a vessel. And he said unto her, there is not a vessel more. And the oil stayed. Then she came and told the man of God. And he said, Go, sell the oil, and pay thy debt, and live thou and thy children of the rest." (2 Kings 4:1-7, KJV)

SECURING YOUR FUTURE

He died leaving behind a huge debt and the creditors wanted to take his sons from his widow to make them slaves. (That was allowed in those days). The helpless widow ran to Elisha for help. Thank God she ran to a man of God who was sensitive to the Spirit of God and knew the solution for the hour. Elisha asked her, "Tell me, what do you have in your house?" I am asking you the same question, "What do you have in your hand?" Because it is what is within your reach that God is going to use to bless you.

You already have the solution with you. Often, we think the solution is in a faraway place. Let us be very sincere, when you are trusting God to prosper you or give you a breakthrough, most people imagine that God will send somebody from abroad who will provide resources to start a business. Yes, He can do that, however most times God's answer is within our reach and unless our eyes are opened, we are sure to miss it.

In addition, for God to prosper you from what you are doing right now, you may have to change the way you are doing it or add something to it. You cannot continue to do the same thing the way you have always done it and expect something different. It will not happen! At best God will reward your diligence and you will have enough to eat. That is happening to a lot of very hardworking people you see around who are not listening to or following God's direction for their lives. They work so hard but several years later, they are still more or less at the same level. You must seek His guidance and do some research on how you can do it better. You must allow God to lead you in whatever you do to reduce wastages or losses in your life. That is the surest way to make something secure.

What does it really mean to secure something? It means to guard it, to make it safe, or to ensure it is protected. So, what are you protecting your future from when making it secure? You are protecting it against loss, danger, risk, failure, destruction etc.

For instance, let's say you have two wristwatches, you bought one of them at a cheap price from a discount shop and the other one is an original designer wristwatch that comes with its own special case, which you received as a birthday present. Would you treat the two wristwatches the same way? Most likely not. You would probably ensure that the second one is well secured and protected. When you know that people in your house or your office typically dump things that they do not really want on a shelf, you would certainly not leave the designer wristwatch on that shelf. You would not want to take the chance because the wristwatch is precious to you. You will do your best to protect it from any damage because you intend to save it for a special occasion in the future, or a day when you will really need it.

Have you ever heard stories of people who bought land in a remote place when it was just a few thousand Dollars? At that time, the land was situated in a forest that required at least a travel time of about three hours before getting there. Today, that area is now seen as a choice piece of property and the land has now become unbelievably valuable.

I was once told the story of a businessman who was working somewhere in Nigeria before he was posted out of the country. But before he left, he put all his money together and even took out a loan to buy a piece of land in a remote location. At that time, the land cost about $1,250, which was a lot of money back then. He paid for the land, travelled abroad, and then forgot about it.

He returned to Nigeria about four years later. By the time he returned, there were people who were ready to buy the land from him and were begging him to accept $100,000 for it. He even expected to be paid even more money for the land. So, he turned down the offer of $100,000 because that land had now become one of the most exclusive areas in the country. Yet, he had bought it at $1,250. That money was sitting idle in the bank waiting to be sent on an errand until this man decided to make that move. It is not as though he could not have used the money for something else. He could have used it to enjoy himself like many of us like to do, but he chose to invest the money. He closed his eyes to pleasure and four years later, he was being offered, or rather, he was being begged to accept $100,000 for a land he bought just for $1,250.

That is an example of financial security. The Lord will teach us how to secure our future. Why is it important for us to discuss this? It is because the things that previously used to make men secure, have begun to crumble around us.

Proverbs 27 verse 24 says,

"For riches are not for ever: and doth the crown endure to every generation?" (Proverbs 27:24, KJV)

There are some celebrity names we heard constantly in the 1960s, 1970s and 1980s that we no longer hear about anymore. In those days, popular musicians such as Sunny Ade and Ebenezer Obey would praise these celebrities at parties and their heads would swell with pride at their accomplishments. They would empty their wallets in appreciation to these musicians. Some of those celebrities are still alive today, but you hardly hear their names being mentioned anymore. Such riches are not forever, the only type of riches that will last forever are the ones given by God.

Let us reflect on the story of the good man that leaves behind riches not just for his children but even for his children's children to inherit. Ask yourself, "What can I leave behind that my children or the ones I shall have will inherit?"

Some people may leave behind houses, land, company shares for their children. However, if it is a quality education that you give to your children as their inheritance, then you have given them a good platform to build on even after you are gone. More importantly, if you can back this education with an intimate knowledge of God and His ways and they follow those Godly principles, you would have helped them to secure their future.

The Bible states in Proverbs 22:6,

"Train up a child in the way he should go: and when he is old, he will not depart from it." (Proverbs 22:6, KJV)

Leaving lands, houses, or company shares are not enough in securing your children's future. If your grandfather who died many years ago left a house for you, would you want to live there today? That house would probably be incredibly old. It may have been a nice-looking mansion when they built it in the 1960s or 1970s, but it would likely be old fashioned by now. Since you still have the land, you may choose to pull down the building and build something more modern but that is a whole lot of money that you would be forced to spend. Owning a house is not enough security for your children's future.

Let us look at Psalm 34:12:

"What man is he that desireth life, and loveth many days, that he may see good?" (Psalms 34:12, KJV)

If you are in the shoes of that person and things are going very well for you in life, you would certainly want Jesus to tarry some more. But the person that is living from hand to mouth every day would likely be praying that the Lord should come quickly to the earth and for the End to come.

Do you know God's plan for yourself and for your family for the next year, two years, maybe even the next twenty years to come? A plan is not the same as a dream. The desire to buy a car, build a house, or travel around the world is not a plan but a dream. A plan is a series of steps or actions that you intend to take in a systematic way to accomplish what you desire. For example, this is what I will do in five or ten years to achieve this or that. But when it comes to dreams, it is easy to dream. If you want, you can daydream for one or two hours. You can build a mansion and decorate all the rooms daydreaming.

A dream is just a desire except it is planted by God himself. The Bible says that in the multitude of businesses, dreams appear, so it is easy to desire things. But when it comes to making plans, it requires work. What is your plan for the next five, ten or twenty years? Those plans may frighten you. Honestly, if they are inspired by God, they will frighten you because they will be beyond your own ability.

Some years ago, I was thinking about the school education of my children and I started drawing up a plan. I was scared because it was obvious that from what I could see, we could not afford it because of the high cost. So, I left that plan and I did not look at it for nearly two years.

Imagine you are in Joseph's shoes. You are the second to the last child of your father, your mum has died, and you have elder brothers who are doing well. You then dream that you will be above them all, that they will all bow down to you.

How would you have felt? Wouldn't you ask yourself if it would be possible? You may think it is impossible, but if any dream is of God, no matter how big, be assured that it would come to pass provided you do your part. We serve a big God. May the Lord give us all big dreams. He will help us. He will give us the wisdom to work to make those dreams come to pass in Jesus' name. Amen.

Now let us look at Proverbs 29:18, it says:

"Where there is no vision, the people perish: but he that keepeth the law, happy is he." (Proverbs 29:18, KJV)

Someone said it is only a foolish man that will keep doing the same thing the same way and will expect different results. If you have a vision, you need to modify the way you do things so that you will get the result you expect.

Phil 3:13-14 states that,

"Brethren, I count not myself to have apprehended: but this one thing I do, forgetting those things which are behind, and reaching forth unto those things which are before, I press toward the mark for the prize of the high calling of God in Christ Jesus." (Philippians 3:13-14, KJV)

Pressing forward suggests that there are obstacles or barriers to your progress. As you overcome one obstacle or achieve something, thank God, and continue to move on. Do not be too comfortable when you achieve success at a certain step so that you stay on the mountain and no longer bother to continue to make progress. For instance, a sister may be trusting God for a life partner. Apart from praying, she also takes really good care of her appearance. Then God gives her the man and she gets married. Rather than continue to maintain her appearance, she no longer cares and gets out of shape, going from size 8 to 10, from 10 to 12 to 14. She is no longer pressing forward. She may also start putting aside especially important things such as the work of God because she is no longer under pressure, having realised her dream of getting married.

A couple may have a dream of building a house or doing something for God, but they put it aside saying, "I now have many mouths to feed." You should feed your family but do not allow your dreams to die. Continue to challenge yourself towards the accomplishment of those dreams.

SECURING YOUR FUTURE

God's system will secure your future. As you look to Him and follow His word, your future and the future of your children's children will be secured in Jesus' name.

Prayer

Father I look to you, teach me how to secure my future in Jesus' name. Amen.

Chapter Two

Following The Right Path To Success

There are right and wrong ways to achieve success. As believers we need to identify the right or Godly ways and to avoid the wrong ways. The Bible states in Prov. 14:12

"There is a way which seemeth right unto a man, but the end thereof are the ways of death." (Proverbs 14:12, KJV)

May you discern the right way to succeed in every area of your life in Jesus' name.

Steps to take towards your plan

What steps are you taking now that will bring you closer to your plan? Many of us have plans but we have not written them down yet. You are encouraged in Habakkuk 2:1-3 to wait on the Lord and to write down your plans.

It states that,

"I will stand upon my watch, and set me upon the tower, and will watch to see what he will say unto me, and what I shall answer when I am reproved. And the LORD answered me, and said, Write the vision, and make it plain upon tables, that he may run that

readeth it. For the vision is yet for an appointed time, but at the end it shall speak, and not lie: though it tarry, wait for it; because it will surely come, it will not tarry." (Habakkuk 2:1-3, KJV)

You just have a picture of it in your mind. What steps are you taking right now towards that plan?

Let us look at two other scriptures:

"If they obey and serve him, they shall spend their days in prosperity, and their years in pleasures." (Job 36:11, KJV)

"If ye be willing and obedient, ye shall eat the good of the land:" (Isaiah 1:19, KJV)

According to Job 36:11, obedience and service to God are prerequisites for the prosperity of believers. Do you know what God has asked you to do? Are you obeying God? Are you serving God?

Isaiah 1:19 says that your obedience to God must be something you do willingly, not grudgingly. If you willingly obey God, even during a financial meltdown, God will ensure you partake of the best in a country that is ravaged by an economic downturn. You will eat the goodness of the land and you will get it legitimately and not through fraudulent means.

Steps that can draw you away from your plan

Another question you need to ask yourself is what steps am I taking now that can drive me further away from God's plan for my life? Maybe you cannot readily identify any wrong thing you are doing, but there are some negative steps that can delay or prevent the actualisation of your plans.

One ready example is procrastination, which is the thief of time. The person keeps postponing what can be done till a future date. You hear them say, "I will do it tomorrow; I will do it the day after." The lazy man will get up and say, "There is a lion in the street." I will not be able to go out today.

"A slothful man saith, there is a lion without, I shall be slain in the streets." (Proverbs 22:13, KJV)

The Bible says he is slothful. What happens to slothful men ? Poverty comes upon them like a vagabond. Anyone who is slothful will not make progress in life even if he is given all the opportunities in life. Even people that are not given such opportunities will eventually overtake him.

A cousin of mine once told me a story. Many years ago, when they were in school, he had a friend who was the only son of his father. In those days, his father bought him a brand-new Peugeot 504 car. Back then, that used to be the reigning car. His father also gave him a house to live in. My cousin spotted his friend on the road ten years later, pushing the car. His friend was still driving that same car. That car had broken down many times and had repeatedly been repaired, but this man was still driving around a ten-year-old car!

By that time, many of his mates who never received such opportunities as he had in school were driving around in brand new cars. When my cousin's friend had received his car back then, many people thought that he had gone far ahead of them in life because not everyone's parents could afford to buy them a car or give them a house. However, much later in life, the story turned out to be different.

We need to secure our children's future by teaching them to be godly and to do the things that please the Lord. Though the father of the man did well by leaving assets for his son, he apparently did not teach him how to multiply what he was leaving for him. This situation is as though people are in a race and at the beginning, they place someone in front of the other runners.

SECURING YOUR FUTURE

That person can run ahead of others but once he relaxes, others can and will catch up with him and even get ahead of him. If you succeed at running ahead of others or you are successful in any way, ensure that you pass the baton to your children and your children's children in the right way.

Another thing that you can do that drives you further away from your plan is selling your birthright, or not valuing what God has done in your life or the position he has placed you in. For us as Christians, our birthright is our salvation, which gives us access to God. The Bible says that all things are yours and you are Christ's.

The Bible also says that He has raised us up and placed us in the heavenly places in Christ. When you know what God wants you to do in any situation and you refuse to do it, when you compromise your values or grieve the Holy Spirit in any way, you are essentially selling your birthright and giving in to the kingdom of darkness.

In your place of work, your Christian values should be clear not just by the things you say, but by your lifestyle. If you collect bribes or exhibit pride or engage in ungodly behaviour, you will not be able to bind and loose, or exercise your spiritual authority. You will not be able to use Godly principles to excel at your work. By joining unbelievers to participate in unethical practices at your place of work or school, you are depriving yourself of the special privileges you are expected to have in Christ.

The Bible talks of beggars that are riding on horses and princes that are walking on the ground.

"Folly is set in great dignity, and the rich sit in low place. I have seen servants upon horses, and princes walking as servants upon the earth." (Ecclesiastes 10:6-7, KJV)

That is not how it should be, but that can happen when we sell our birthright. If Christians compromise their stand in God, unbelievers can continue getting the good things that should be coming to the Christians.

Another thing that can keep us away from our plan is the way we handle our finances. If someone earns $300 per month and pays rent of $100 monthly, he is left with $200. If his brother in the village comes and he gives him $30 he is left with $170. If he decides to go and borrow because the income, he has left is not enough to take care of all his other needs, by the next month, the money he has borrowed will eat deep into his salary. Yet, he still has the other regular monthly expenses. Then he tells himself that what he has left is so little that he cannot give offering or pay the correct tithe. Instead of giving $30 as tithe, he gives $10 telling himself he will meet up next month, what is he doing? He is eating his seed.

Biblical nuggets to securing your future

Let us consider some nuggets from the Bible that will guide us in securing our future:

One of the very first things that you must do to secure your future is to **choose to do things God's way.**

Take time to know and understand the will of God for your life. Obtain scriptures from the Lord and meditate on them. Joshua 1:7–8 states,

"Only be thou strong and very courageous, that thou mayest observe to do according to all the law, which Moses my servant commanded thee: turn not from it to the right hand or to the left, that thou mayest prosper whithersoever thou goest. This book of the law shall not depart out of thy mouth; but thou shalt meditate therein day and night, that thou mayest observe to do according to all that is written therein: for then thou shalt make thy way

prosperous, and then thou shalt have good success." (Joshua 1:7-8, KJV)

If it is the way God wants you to do it, ensure you do it that way. It may cost you something, it could even be painful, but you are securing your future. Jesus says in John 14:6,

"Jesus saith unto him, I am the way, the truth, and the life: no man cometh unto the Father, but by me." (John 14:6, KJV)

Find out from Him the right way to go. He knows the right way for you to succeed.

The second most important thing in securing your future is to **submit to God.**

Submit yourself to God, humble yourself, and He will honour you in due season. Submission is tough but it is rewarding. When you are submitting to God, some people will think that you are being foolish, but just continue doing it. You will eventually reach your breakthrough point.

In the Bible, it did not make sense for Isaac to stay and sow in a land of famine. He did not want to do so, but he instead chose to submit his will to God's way and his life completely changed because of his submission. May your life change for the better as you submit to the will of God for your life in Jesus' name.

The third most important thing in securing your future is that you should **be ready to face challenges.**

He that watches the wind will not sow. The time will never be right for you to do whatever you need to do to secure your future. There will always be other reasons or circumstances that will arise to prevent you from taking a step of faith. I had an aunt who had this saying about people who always claim they do not have to give: "I don't have enough; I don't have enough is what turns a man into a miser." She said people who always claim that the reason they do not give is because they have so little will also not give in future if they have $1000. If you are finding it difficult to pay your tithe or give the little offering you have now, even when you earn $5000 from a contract, you will give God thousands of reasons why you cannot give ten percent.

Luke 6:38 states,

"Give, and it shall be given unto you; good measure, pressed down, and shaken together, and running over, shall men give into your bosom. For with the same measure that ye mete withal it shall be measured to you again." (Luke 6:38, KJV)

The fourth important thing in securing your future is that you should **learn to give.**

Do not withhold your seed anytime you have an opportunity to give because you do not know which of your seeds will prosper or whether all will prosper. Ecclesiastes 11:6 says,

"In the morning sow thy seed, and in the evening withhold not thine hand: for thou knowest not whether shall prosper, either this or that, or whether they both shall be alike good." (Ecclesiastes 11:6, KJV)

If people know of a special ministry that if they sow their money, they will get a hundredfold return and enjoy an exceptionally long life, they will practically queue up to bless that ministry. In this same way, you should continue to do good because you do not know which of your good deeds will speak for you and at what time. Just continue to sow time, money, prayers, even if it is in tears. Ps 126:6 states,

"He that goeth forth and weepeth, bearing precious seed, shall doubtless come again with rejoicing, bringing his sheaves with him." (Psalms 126:6, KJV)

SECURING YOUR FUTURE

You do not know which one of your seeds will speak for you. Mordecai, in the book of Esther, had done a good deed for the king but he was not given any reward at that time. But much later in life, because of what he did for the king, the book of remembrance was opened. Mordecai had unknowingly, been storing up things for himself, for the day of remembrance. It was just that it happened to be one of his deeds that caught the king's attention. But in the eyes of God, it was an accumulation of everything he had previously done.

I know of a man of God who used to earn a miniscule income many years ago. There were three key ministers in his parish that worked full time. Every month after collecting his salary, he would first pay his tithe from his income and then he would put money in three separate envelopes for each of the ministers. He did this every month for about 6 months, and it was after giving that he would begin to spend the little he had left. Till this day, I can testify about what God did and is still doing in his life. The places that he would not even have dreamed that he would get to, he is getting there. Therefore, sow at every opportunity since you do not know which one will work for you, just sow.

However, some grounds are fertile grounds. You do not need anybody or an angel to tell you that this is fertile ground when you see one. But you must be diligent in your work as you will one day stand before kings, not before mere, ordinary men. I recently read a book, Outliers (The Story of Success) by Malcolm Gladwell, which blew my mind. Gladwell is a scientist. He observes what is happening around him and studies natural phenomenon. I recommend that you should get the book to read. Gladwell took the example of Bill Gates and other individuals that are successful in their fields. He showed that the success they experience is not because they came from the best homes or attended the best schools. Rather, their advantage is twofold: one, they were all in the right place at the right time when things were happening and two, they spent a lot of time practising. Gladwell discovered that these individuals spent at least ten thousand hours of their life practising before they became particularly good at what they were doing.

How many hours are there in a day? 24 hours. Out of that, one must sleep, one must eat and go to school and/or work. So, the spare hours that we are left with cannot be more than four or five. Calculate four or five hours over many years. By the time the author calculated it, it showed that these successful people had spent at least six to seven hours a day practising their endeavours over a period of about five years. Let nobody say it was because their parents were wealthy, or that their success was due to the schools they attended, because other people attended these same schools and were not so successful.

Gladwell also talked about a musical group that used to go to Germany. They would practise all night long from 8pm till 6am for more than two years. He was trying to prove that practice makes perfect. After doing this for several years, they became one of the most famous bands and released some of the highest-selling albums in the world (up till today). If you are diligent at what you do and you keep doing it well, there is no way you will not succeed.

The problem for many of us is that we get tired too quickly. If you observe life on a high street, you will notice that for the people who operate businesses there usually leave, and in a short while they are replaced by other people who take over the shop. These people complain that things are hard and that their business is not thriving. They give various excuses and reasons for failing.

Many people have delved into businesses such as the production of sachet water because they saw others doing it, but left the business because it was not as profitable as they had thought. But when you look at many multinational companies today, you will discover that many of them were started about fifty years ago, or even earlier. These businesses have persisted despite the various challenges that they have faced over the years. They succeeded because they were consistent and committed to delivering superior products and services.

Some people really need to change their jobs, but they continue to observe the wind. Since they have heard that many companies are no longer employing these days, they tell themselves, "I shouldn't think of changing my job." But even in periods of economic downturn, some people are still getting hired. Even as people are being fired, others are being employed. Companies still need certain skills, so you need to upgrade yourself to acquire the necessary skills that will make companies seek out your services. If you observe the wind, you may not do anything about your future. Even at periods of terrible economic hardship, you can prosper if you obey God's instructions.

There was famine in the land, but Isaac prospered exceedingly. Jacob also prospered but he served before he prospered. He was diligent. He served seven years to get Rachel the woman he loved but the father-in-law played pranks and he had to serve another seven years. He served very well so when Laban, his father in-law decided to separate the flock, hoping to cheat Jacob, God still ensured that Jacob came out successful.

The fifth point to securing your future is to **be creative.**

Think, dream, and receive big visions from God. Isaiah 54 verse 2 says:

"Enlarge the place of thy tent, and let them stretch forth the curtains of thine habitations: spare not, lengthen thy cords, and strengthen thy stakes;" (Isaiah 54:2, KJV)

Expand any good thing you are doing. Do not restrict your success to where you are living or working. Push the boundaries. Do not limit yourself. Go the extra mile. Many people leave the village and move to the city, but they are still parochial and narrow-minded in their thinking. When we limit ourselves, it is as though we are holding God back. We are restricting His hand, not allowing Him to take us to where He wants us to be. To enlarge your tent, you need to dream big and to have big visions. If you are earning $250 today, bless God for it but make plans to earn about $1000 in the next three years. Do not limit yourself by making plans to earn only about $350 in three years' time. However, do not let your plan be based on fraudulent practices in your office. Do not also base your plan on the struggles of the workers' union in your place of work.

When the union struggles for salary increase, the management will only add a little amount, like $50 per month. The union may make further demands and the management would probably add less than $50. Do not depend on the supposed kindness of the management, instead endeavour to enlarge your tent. When you have decided to earn $1000 monthly within that period, do not simply sit down and expect that amount to materialise. Challenge yourself and go to the Lord in prayers.

Before the sky breaks forth with rain, you must first load it, and load it, and load it again and again. How are you loading your sky? If you expect a downpour, you must start working towards it. When I read the Outliers book, I thought of Pastor E.A. Adeboye. He spends at least four hours in the night praying and studying his Bible. Is it any wonder that he is where he is today? Through him, God does many mighty miracles even for those who do not seem to deserve it.

Great blessings come from being diligent and persevering. What we all need is vision to direct us. We need to continue sowing. We cannot tell which of our efforts will result in fruits.

I want to challenge you to find time to go through the Bible and search out two examples of people who secured their future. Study the Bible to see what they did to secure their future. There must be something you can learn from them. One clear thing that you will discover is that they refused to give up on God or on the possibility of a better future. Starting from Genesis, some of the popular examples include Abraham, Joseph, David, Nehemiah, and Daniel. They are people who not only prospered, but also did things to secure their future. Abraham responded when God told him to count the stars in the sky. God told him that is how innumerable his offspring would be.

Isaac and Jacob are also men who secured their future by obeying God. Jabez was a man who told God, "Enlarge my coast." Did God answer him? Yes. He changed his story to a happy one. Japheth in Genesis 9:21-27 secured his future. His brother saw their father's nakedness and came to tell him. He and another brother of his went in walking backwards so as not to see their father's nakedness and covered him. In verse 27, his father prayed for him, "May God enlarge Japheth, and may he dwell in the tents of Shem; And may Canaan be his servant." The Bible did not tell us what work Japheth had been doing, but just for that single act God enlarged him and his brother Canaan served him. There are singular acts that provoke generational blessings. By doing such things you would not only be securing your own future but the future of many generations in your lineage.

There are also acts that you must do diligently and consistently every day to secure your future. Always ask God to cause your seed to speak for you both now and in the future. You do not know which seed God will use to avert the evil that is on your way. You do not know the person that you will help who will be the one praying for you on the day you need prayer. It could be that you are already getting weary and God stirs up the person to pray for you so that you will be able to withstand the challenge you are facing.

Finally, **be thankful to God for all things.**

1 Thessalonians 5:18 says,

"In everything give thanks: for this is the will of God in Christ Jesus concerning you." (1 Thessalonians 5:18, KJV)

For whatever you can achieve at whatever level, learn to live a life of appreciation and thanksgiving to God.

Prayer

Father show me the way to walk and the thing I must do to secure my future in Jesus' name. Amen.

Chapter Three

Making Godly Decisions

The man who will secure his future must learn how to make godly decisions. In this chapter we will do an X-ray of the life of Isaac, the son of Abraham who in Genesis chapter 26 received abundance from God and secured the future of his family even during an economic meltdown. What was so special about him? What did he do? What can we learn from him? Isaac heard from God and made a quality decision for his life even when it did not make sense to do so.

The financial situation you are experiencing is not new

"And there was a famine in the land, beside the first famine that was in the days of Abraham. And Isaac went unto Abimelech king of the Philistines unto Gerar." (Genesis 26:1, KJV)

Isaac faced a famine and before him and after him there were other famines. You are not the first person to pass through a financial challenge. As you go through the Scriptures and as you read the local newspapers, you will see that there are stories of famines, earthquakes, floods, and more disasters rendering thousands of people homeless and facing financial challenges. It was like that in Biblical times, such as in Isaac's time, and it is still happening today. Most of these people who face these challenges did not choose the challenge that came across their way, it was sprung on them. You cannot always determine what happens to you or around you. However, you have a choice to decide how to respond to what happens to you. When you choose to listen to the voice of God as Isaac did and to respond using Biblical principles that have worked, you also will become a victor. May you be victorious over every challenge you are facing right now in the name of Jesus.

When you face a challenge, the instinct is to run for help or to check out

Isaac and his family packed their luggage and instinctively began to head for Egypt when the famine struck. His reaction was completely normal and the way of the world. He was running away in search of help. What is your personal experience when you run to others for help? Those you run to for help often fail you. Often, those you are looking to for assistance tend to fail you. The Bible tells us in Jeremiah 17:5-6,

"Thus, saith the LORD; Cursed be the man that trusteth in man, and maketh flesh his arm, and whose heart departeth from the LORD. For he shall be like the heath in the desert, and shall not see when good cometh; but shall inhabit the parched places in the wilderness, in a salt land and not inhabited." (Jeremiah 17:5-6, KJV)

The man who relies on his fellow man for help is cursed. May you not be cursed in Jesus' name. We should not follow the direction of the world but run to Jesus. In His Word are answers for every challenge we face. In Matthew 11: 28-30,

"Come unto me, all ye that labour and are heavy laden, and I will give you rest. Take my yoke upon you and learn of me; for I am meek and lowly in heart: and ye shall find rest unto your souls. For my yoke is easy, and my burden is light." (Matthew 11:28-30, KJV)

Jesus gave an open invitation to exchange our burdens for His rest. May you seize this opportunity in Jesus' name.

Recognize that direction comes from God

"And the LORD appeared unto him, and said, Go not down into Egypt; dwell in the land which I shall tell thee of: Sojourn in this land, and I will be with thee, and will bless thee; for unto thee, and unto thy seed, I will give all these countries, and I will perform the oath which I sware unto Abraham thy father; And I will make thy seed to multiply as the stars of heaven, and will give unto thy seed all these countries; and in thy seed shall all the nations of the earth be blessed; Because that Abraham obeyed my voice, and kept my charge, my commandments, my statutes, and my laws." (Genesis 26:2-5, KJV)

When the Lord saw Isaac running away towards Egypt, He immediately spoke to him, told him where to stay and promised to bless him and to bless his generation. I believe that the covenant relationship that Abraham had with God contributed to the Lord's intervention in Isaac's runaway plans. Thank God that Isaac was also sensitive to hear the voice of God. Has God spoken to you before? How does He speak to you? When did you hear from Him last? How do you know when it is the Lord speaking? May the Lord activate your discerning 'equipment' that you may hear Him when He speaks to you in Jesus' name.

Obedience to Godly direction is vital for your survival

"And Isaac dwelt in Gerar:" (Genesis 26:6, KJV)

Isaac chose to obey God. This was a quality decision that was vital to his survival. The blessings of obedience cannot be quantified. The Bible has many examples of characters who chose to obey God even when it did not seem right. Obedience to God always has benefits for today and for the future. May you learn to obey God in Jesus' name.

Avoid distractions

"And the men of the place asked him of his wife; and he said, She is my sister: for he feared to say, She is my wife; lest, said he, the men of the place should kill me for Rebekah; because she was fair to look upon. And it came to pass, when he had been there a long time, that Abimelech king of the Philistines looked out at a window, and saw, and behold, Isaac was sporting with Rebekah his wife. And Abimelech called Isaac, and said, Behold, of a surety she is thy wife: and how saidst thou, she is my sister? And Isaac said unto him, Because I said, Lest I die for her. And Abimelech said, what is this thou hast done unto us? one of the people might lightly have lien with thy wife, and thou shouldest have brought guiltiness upon us. And Abimelech charged all his people, saying, He that toucheth this man or his wife shall surely be put to death." (Genesis 26:7-11, KJV)

When God is set to do a new or special thing in your life, the enemy tends to use things or objects to distract our attention from what the Lord has in stock for us. Isaac was distracted by the men of the land who enquired about his beautiful wife. In a bid to protect himself he lied. Distractions can come in the form of lies, deceit, the lust of the eyes, the lust of the flesh or the pride of life.

"Neither give place to the devil." (Ephesians 4:27, KJV)

The objective of the devil is to cause you to take your eyes away from God's plan or purpose for your life so that you miss out on God's plan for your life In Isaiah 26:3

"Thou wilt keep him in perfect peace, whose mind is stayed on thee: because he trusteth in thee." (Isaiah 26:3, KJV)

The Bible promises that we would be kept in perfect peace if we maintain our focus on Him. May you not be distracted from the plan and purpose of God for your life in Jesus' name.

Sow in the land

"Then Isaac sowed in that land, and received in the same year an hundredfold: and the LORD blessed him." (Genesis 26:12, KJV)

Isaac defied all odds and he sowed, planted, cultivated, worked hard, laboured where the Lord had asked him to stay even though it was not convenient. Despite the obvious difficulties, Isaac walked by faith and in obedience to the word of God. He planted seeds on a difficult terrain in conditions that were unbearable. Are you where the Lord asked you to be? Did you check with him before you moved to your current location? What does it mean to defy all odds? To do whatever God has asked you to do no matter how difficult it seems? What is the Lord asking you to do right now? Have you done it? Follow the example of Isaac and take a step of faith in obedience and prepare to reap an abundant harvest.

Obedience leads to fruitfulness

"And the man waxed great, and went forward, and grew until he became very great: For he had possession of flocks, and possession of herds, and great store of servants: and the Philistines envied him." (Genesis 26:13-14, KJV)

In the place of obedience there is fruitfulness. The result of Isaac's obedience led to all round fruitfulness. The person who had been running away from the famine in the land suddenly became associated with greatness, progress, growth, abundance, multiplication, higher levels, with lots of cattle and servants. He became an envy to his neighbours. May the result of your obedience attract divine promotion, and may you be the envy of your neighbours in the name of Jesus.

Ignore oppositions and remain focused

"For all the wells which his father's servants had digged in the days of Abraham his father, the Philistines had stopped them, and filled them with earth. And Abimelech said unto Isaac, Go from us; for thou art much mightier than we." (Genesis 26:15-16, KJV)

Opposition comes even when you are in the will of God. Although Isaac was following the instruction of the Lord, he faced stiff opposition from the Philistines. Examples abound in the Scriptures of opposition to the will of God. Opposition that comes when you are in the will of God will eventually give way to your victory in Jesus' name. The Bible says in Romans 8:31,

"What shall we then say to these things? If God be for us, who can be against us?" (Romans 8:31, KJV)

If God be for us who can be against us. The Lord will make you more than a conqueror in Jesus' name.

Be persistent. Do not give up

"And Isaac departed thence, and pitched his tent in the valley of Gerar, and dwelt there. And Isaac digged again the wells of water, which they had digged in the days of Abraham his father; for the Philistines had stopped them after the death of Abraham: and he called their names after the names by which his father had called them. And Isaac's servants digged in the valley and found there a well of springing water. And the herdmen of Gerar did strive with Isaac's herdmen, saying, the water is ours: and he called the name of the well Esek; because they strove with him. And they digged another well and strove for that also: and he called the name of it Sitnah. And he removed from thence, and digged another well; and for that they strove not: and he called the name of it Rehoboth; and he said, For now the LORD hath made room for us, and we shall be fruitful in the land." (Genesis 26:17-22, KJV)

Isaac did not give up. As they blocked his wells, he kept moving from one well to the other. Whenever the Philistines came to close his wells, he moved on from one location to another. Persistence, diligence, and hard work even in the face of difficulties will eventually be rewarded. Remember to maintain the right confession and profession throughout until your breakthrough emerges.

When you are in God's will, your enemies will eventually acknowledge the favour of God on your life. At the end of the difficult circumstances, the Philistines had no choice but to acknowledge the hand of God upon the life of Isaac.

"When a man's ways please the LORD, he maketh even his enemies to be at peace with him." (Proverbs 16:7, KJV)

When a man's ways please the Lord, his enemies are at peace with him. I am confident that the Lord will reassure you, comfort you, strengthen you, and give you victory over that situation in Jesus' name.

Load your sky continually

Finally, before the sky breaks forth with rain, you must make a quality decision or choice to first load it. Ecclesiastes 11:3 says,

"If the clouds be full of rain, they empty themselves upon the earth: and if the tree fall toward the south, or toward the north, in the place where the tree falleth, there it shall be." (Ecclesiastes 11:3, KJV)

The clouds cannot deliver the rain they have not conceived. Many times, believers expect the downpour of blessings without necessarily working towards it. It does not work like that. If you fail to load your clouds, you will continue to be in dryness. Therefore, you need to continue to sow and sow.

You cannot tell which sowing time will deliver a bountiful harvest. The Bible states in Ecclesiastes 11:1-6,

"Cast thy bread upon the waters: for thou shalt find it after many days. Give a portion to seven, and also to eight; for thou knowest not what evil shall be upon the earth. If the clouds be full of rain, they empty themselves upon the earth: and if the tree fall toward the south, or toward the north, in the place where the tree falleth, there it shall be. He that observeth the wind shall not sow; and he that regardeth the clouds shall not reap. As thou knowest not what is the way of the spirit, nor how the bones do grow in the womb of her that is with child: even so thou knowest not the works of God who maketh all. In the morning sow thy seed, and in the evening withhold not thine hand: for thou knowest not whether shall prosper, either this or that, or whether they both shall be alike good." (Ecclesiastes 11:1-6, KJV)

In addition, ask God to use your seeds to avert evil from your path. Remember, God's way is the only way to navigate, survive and to thrive when you are going through financial difficulties. As you walk closely with the Lord, He will show you where to stay and what actions to take. Your role is to hear Him well and to walk in obedience to his leading.

Prayer

Father use my seed to avert evil from my life in Jesus' name. Amen.

Chapter Four

Adopting The Right Attitude For Your Success

The person who will secure his or her future must adopt a right attitude to guarantee success even in the face of extreme difficulty and hardship. 2 Kings 4: 1-7

"Now there cried a certain woman of the wives of the sons of the prophets unto Elisha, saying, Thy servant my husband is dead; and thou knowest that thy servant did fear the LORD: and the creditor is come to take unto him my two sons to be bondmen. And Elisha said unto her, what shall I do for thee? tell me, what hast thou in the house? And she said, thine handmaid hath not anything in the house, save a pot of oil. Then he said, Go, borrow thee vessels abroad of all thy neighbours, even empty vessels; borrow not a few. And when thou art come in, thou shalt shut the door upon thee and upon thy sons, and shalt pour out into all those vessels, and thou shalt set aside that which is full. So, she went from him, and shut the door upon her and upon her sons, who brought the vessels to her; and she poured out. And it came to pass, when the vessels were full, that she said unto her son, Bring me yet a vessel. And he said unto her, there is not a vessel more. And the oil stayed. Then she came and told the man of God.

And he said, Go, sell the oil, and pay thy debt, and live thou and thy children of the rest." (2 Kings 4:1-7, KJV)

It tells the story of a woman who was confronted with a huge debt that her late husband left behind. It came to a point that the people whom the man owed wanted to take her children in exchange for the debt until she paid back.

The widow in this chapter realised that she could not help the situation and if she were not careful the matter would get out of hand. She did not murmur or panic or rant, instead she adopted the attitude of looking to God for help. She ran to the man of God, and the man of God asked her, "What do you have in your house?" Her first response was nothing, then she remembered that she had a little oil in a jar. The man of God gave her some instructions. By following the instructions of the man of God, she was able to pay off the debt by selling the oil.

There is something remarkably interesting about the story as the Bible says that her husband was one of the sons of a prophet. His status did not prevent him from being in debt. He was apparently under the oppression of the devil in his lifetime through poverty and it would have continued in the lives of his children if not for the intervention of the Lord.

Why did the son of the prophet not seek God's intervention in his lifetime and put a stop to it? We do not know. Apparently, there are Christians who for one reason or the other do not put a stop to the oppression of the devil in their lives because they refuse to act. It is possible for one to be a professing Christian and still be poor. You can be a professing Christian and your marriage is not secured. You can be a professing Christian and have ill health or sickness in your body. The deceased was a son of a prophet. The Bible says that the deceased feared the Lord. Despite that, he was still under the bondage of poverty. All these issues should make you ask yourself, "How secure is my future?" You can categorise your future into – your financial future, your marital future, your children's future, your career future, your ministry future etc.

Let us start with our financial future. Some of us are living from pay cheque to pay cheque. For some of us, our pay gets exhausted before the next pay cheque comes in.

Our marital future is another example. Some of us are experiencing crises in our homes. The husband and wife are not talking to each other. How then do you secure the future of your home or family? How do you secure the future of your job or career? As a result of the economic meltdown, we have heard of people losing their jobs day after day. We should want to secure our future as insurance for tomorrow. No one knows what tomorrow will bring or will give, but what will determine how our tomorrow will be is what we do today or the things we refused to do. Your today will determine what your tomorrow will look like. The life we are living right now is the function of the decisions we made and the life we lived a few days ago, a few weeks ago, or even a few years ago. Unless we get to the point where in the face of hopelessness, we choose to adopt an attitude that looks to God for provision and direction and begin to make decisions that would align with God's words, our future may be insecure.

Proverbs 13:22, says

"A good man leaveth an inheritance to his children's children: and the wealth of the sinner is laid up for the just." (Proverbs 13:22, KJV)

The plan of God for you, for me is not to live from pay cheque to pay cheque, jumping from this business to that business. The plan of God for you is for you to prosper and to leave an inheritance for your children's children. Our financial future is one aspect of our future we need to secure. My father told his children many years ago that he would be the last one to be poor in his lineage. He made a good attempt at securing the future of his children. But I am not sure he went as far as his children's children. But as a professing Christian like the son of the prophet, Elisha's servant, the challenge I am placing before you is that God will grant you grace to secure your future and to leave an inheritance for your children and an inheritance for your children's children. Isaiah 3:10 says,

"Say ye to the righteous, that it shall be well with him: for they shall eat the fruit of their doings." (Isaiah 3:10, KJV)

My father in the Lord, Pastor E.A. Adeboye always say, "my tomorrow shall be alright." I prophesy into your life that your tomorrow shall be alright in the name of Jesus.

So how do we go about securing our future? We shall draw a few points from what the widow of Elisha's servant did. The first thing that I draw out is that she suddenly recognised her situation. But I wonder where she was when the debt was piling up. Is it possible that she did not know her husband was sinking in debt? Is it possible that she knew about the debt but thought it had been settled? Anyway, after her husband's death, she suddenly recognised her situation, that it was a crisis.

You do not have to get to a crisis point before you take the right steps. Either way, when she got to a crisis point, she ran to the man of God. She recognised her situation. You might not be in a crisis today, but you might feel the need from God's word that living from pay cheque to pay cheque is not the plan of God for your life. It could be that you are in debt already and you find it difficult to pay. You may find it difficult to pay your rent, your school fees, or the school fees of your children. That is not the plan of God for your life. You must recognise your current situation, that it is not the will of God for you. The woman recognised her situation and she was prompted and energised to do something about it.

In the Bible, according to Matthew 15:21-28,

"Then Jesus went thence and departed into the coasts of Tyre and Sidon. And behold, a woman of Canaan came out of the same coasts, and cried unto him, saying, Have mercy on me, O Lord, thou Son of David; my daughter is grievously vexed with a devil. But he answered her not a word. And his disciples came and besought him, saying, Send her away; for she crieth after us. But he answered and said, I am not sent but unto the lost sheep of the house of Israel. Then came she and worshipped him, saying, Lord, help me. But he answered and said, It is not meet to take the children's bread, and to cast it to dogs. And she said, Truth, Lord: yet the dogs eat of the crumbs which fall from their masters' table. Then Jesus answered and said unto her, O woman, great is thy faith be it unto thee even as thou wilt. And her daughter was made whole from that very hour." (Matthew 15:21-28, KJV)

There was a woman there who wanted healing for her daughter. According to the laws back then, she did not qualify for the healing because she was Greek. But she ran to Jesus in desperation. When you are desperate for something, it propels you into action. When you are casual about something, it shows in your actions as you will not be serious about taking actions. How casual are you about your future? How desperate are you about your future? That woman was desperate to have her daughter healed and she was not ready to let go until Jesus was ready to heal her daughter. What did Jesus finally say? He said, "Your faith has made your daughter whole." The Bible says the expectation of the righteous will be granted; it will not be cut off. Your desire will be granted. You do not have to be in a crisis to be desperate for a change. All you need to do is to ask yourself, "Where am I today?" and "Where does God want me to be?" and "How am I going to get there?" It might mean that you need to reposition yourself. How then do you reposition yourself? You need to recognise your situation that you are not where you are supposed to be.

SECURING YOUR FUTURE

The widow woman we discussed earlier was not ready to lose her sons because they were very precious to her. The woman mentioned in the previous passage was not ready to lose her daughter. If you owe and the bank wants to take your car or your house or anything that is precious to you, as surety for you to pay your debt, do you know how painful that would be? Very, very painful! But you do not need to wait for that moment. You can do something about your situation now. Do not have the attitude of anything goes, whatever comes. If that is your attitude, then your life would be like a raft on water. Wherever the waves of life move is where your life goes. That is not how the life of a Christian is supposed to be. The life of a Christian should be purposeful. The life of a Christian should be ordered in line with the word of God. The Bible says the steps of a good man are ordered by God.

In securing your life, always remember that there is the way of the world and there is the way of God. Psalm 127:1 says, "Except the Lord build the house, they labour in vain that build it: except the LORD keep the city, the watchman waketh but in vain ." You may have taken an insurance policy to secure your future and the future of your children. You may have insurance covering your home. That is okay. However, the truth is that the things of this world are not secure as we saw recently in the financial markets. It can be up today, and it can crash tomorrow. Your insurance company (or companies) that are alive today can become bankrupt and fold up tomorrow. But the Almighty God never fails. He does not sleep nor slumber. He has not lost any battle and will not lose the battle the enemy may be waging against you in the name of Jesus. So, you need to recognise that and align your life with Him. John 10:10 says,

"The thief cometh not, but for to steal, and to kill, and to destroy: I am come that they might have life, and that they might have it more abundantly." (John 10:10, KJV)

ADOPTING THE RIGHT ATTITUDE FOR YOUR SUCCESS

His desire is that abundant life will be for you and for your children. That is His plan but unless you align with His plan your life remains as it is. In John 15:5, Jesus said, "*I am the vine ye are the branches: He that abideth in me, and I in him, the same bringeth forth much fruit: for without me you can do nothing.*" (*John 15:5, KJV*)

You cannot secure your future without Jesus. Unless you abide with Him, unless you align with Him, unless you run to Him, whatever you do to secure your future will be in vain. In Revelation 1:8, Jesus says,

"*I am Alpha and Omega, the beginning and the ending, saith the Lord, which is, and which was, and which is to come, the Almighty.*" (Revelation 1:8, KJV)

The Almighty knows your end from your beginning. He knows the in between. He knows why He created you. He knows what He created you for. He knows what your future should be. If you decide to align with the one who knows the ending of your life, the one who is actually the beginning and the ending, then your future would be secured.

We have drawn out two points about the widow of one of Elisha's men. The first point is that she recognised her situation and she was desperate to change it. The second thing is that she ran to the man of God to state her problems just as you are to bring the issues of your life to God.

The third point is that the man of God asked her what she had in her house. Her response was that she had nothing but a jar of oil. Most times the Lord gives us whatever we say. Obviously, she had been saying nothing, which reflects what she had experienced. Then to the glory of God she confessed that she had something. Everyone has something that the Lord can use to turn things around. The small boy had five loaves and two fishes. Let your confession align with the word of God. Isaiah 3: 8-11 says,

"For Jerusalem is ruined, and Judah is fallen: because their tongue and their doings are against the LORD, to provoke the eyes of his glory. The shew of their countenance doth witness against them; and they declare their sin as Sodom, they hide it not. Woe unto their soul! for they have rewarded evil unto themselves. Say ye to the righteous, that it shall be well with him: for they shall eat the fruit of their doings. Woe unto the wicked! it shall be ill with him: for the reward of his hands shall be given him." (Isaiah 3:8-11, KJV)

Verse 8 says Jerusalem is in ruin and Judah is falling because their tongue and their doing is against the Lord. They were saying things contrary to God's words, not in line with God's words.

What you say can determine if your future is going to be good or bad. The Bible says in Proverbs 18:21 that death and life are in the power of the tongue. What are you saying about your future? What are the words that are proceeding from your mouth? What do you say concerning yourself? What do you say concerning your children? What do you say concerning your marriage? What do you say concerning your job? What do you say concerning your finances? If you say what the word of God says, then you are aligning yourself for success. If you say something different from God's word, then you are planning for ruin.

In Isaiah 3:8, the Bible states that Jerusalem was ruined. Why? *"For Jerusalem is ruined, and Judah is fallen because their tongue and their doings are against the LORD, to provoke the eyes of his glory."* They said the wrong things. They said things that were not in line with the word of God. May the Lord teach you what to say in the name of Jesus. What you say will inform your future. What you say to your children will inform their future. It was the name that Jabez's mother gave him that suggested the future he was going to have until he became desperate and

ADOPTING THE RIGHT ATTITUDE FOR YOUR SUCCESS

said no. Unless you get to the point where you also say "no, I cannot continue with this", your future may continue in the wrong direction. The Bible says to tell the righteous it shall be well with them. You need to say it to yourself, "It shall be well with me. My tomorrow will be alright. It shall be well with the lives of my children. I shall not lack any good thing." You may be facing challenges, but you have God's word. Say, "I shall not be moved by what I see or what I feel. I shall be moved only by the word of God."

The fourth point is that the man of God gave her specific instructions to go and borrow a lot of vessels from her neighbours and she obeyed. The mother of Jesus at the marriage feast in Cana of Galilee told the servants to obey whatever Jesus tells them to do. John 2:5 says,

"His mother saith unto the servants, Whatsoever he saith unto you, do it." (John 2:5, KJV)

They did and something good occurred. Obedience to God will always result in testimonies.

The fifth thing to note is that she valued people and had an incredibly good relationship with her neighbours, her sons, and of course the man of God. The value she placed on relationships was obvious from the kind of cooperation she obtained from her neighbours and her sons. I want to believe she was a helpful, understanding, and cooperative person. What you value or treasure helps to determine how your life will end. Matthew 6:19-21 says,

"Lay not up for yourselves treasures upon earth, where moth and rust doth corrupt, and where thieves break through and steal: But lay up for yourselves treasures in heaven, where neither moth nor rust doth corrupt, and where thieves do not break through nor steal: For where your treasure is, there will your heart be also." (Matthew 6:19-21, KJV)

SECURING YOUR FUTURE

Where is your treasure? We can have treasure in gold, jewellery, art, and all sorts of items and that is acceptable.

But if you have those and you do not have treasures in heaven, then there is a problem. If you do not value your relationship with your Heavenly Father or your neighbours, it will affect the way you live your life. After all, the Bible encourages us to love God and to love our neighbours as ourselves.

If you are paying your tithe consistently and you have a financial problem, you can go back to your Heavenly Father and say I pay my tithe, "Let the windows of heaven be opened to me." In securing your future, payment of tithe is mandatory; it is your negotiating tool. Recently, a brother told me that he pays his tithe, but that there are times he does not and then he says to God "God, you understand now." I told him at the time, "God will not understand. If you do not pay your tithe regularly, you have been unfaithful." Let it be on record in heaven that you are not a defaulter in the payment of your tithes. When you tender your request to God in times of financial need, you will have Heaven's backing. But if you are a tithe defaulter, your unfaithfulness can stand between you and your request. Philippians 4:15-17 says,

"Now ye Philippians know also, that in the beginning of the gospel, when I departed from Macedonia, no church communicated with me as concerning giving and receiving, but ye only. For even in Thessalonica ye sent once and again unto my necessity. Not because I desire a gift: but I desire fruit that may abound to your account." (Philippians 4:15-17, KJV)

"But I desire fruit that may abound to your account." What does that tell you? You have an account in heaven that you can draw from in time of need. But some people's accounts are in red. Some people have not even created an account in heaven because they have never even made any kingdom investment through tithing. But some people's accounts are mounting up day by day. What kind of account do you have? Where is your

treasure going? Is your treasure going into shares or accumulation of worldly goods? Those are not fully secured. The stock market can be affected by meltdown. Goods can be stolen or destroyed by fire or other things. But there is no financial crisis that can affect your account in heaven, no thief that can break in and steal, and no fire that can consume your heavenly treasure.

To amass treasure for yourself in heaven, the first thing is you need to faithfully pay your tithes. The second thing is you need to be a blessing to the church and to other people through your giving and your relationships with them. Be friendly and helpful. You do not need to have much to be a giver. Jesus said that the widow at the temple who dropped two mites into the offering box had given much more than others who gave large amounts because she gave sacrificially though she had little. When you have a lot to give, give and even when you do not have, also give the little in your hand, because it is your giving that will secure your financial future.

You also need to honour your parents if you want your future to be secured. The man of God was a spiritual father to her, and she honoured him when she ran to see him. Ephesians 6:1-3 says,

"Children obey your parents in the Lord: for this is right. Honour thy father and mother; (which is the first commandment with promise;) that it may be well with thee, and that thou mayest live long on the earth." (Ephesians 6:1-3, KJV)

How have you honoured your parents? What more can you do for your parents as a mark of love and respect that will make them more comfortable? You might not have much, but give something out of what you have. Give to your father and mother. It might be food; it might be money. Find out from them what they need, because when a parent prays for a child, particularly when the child has done something to satisfy them, that blessing is irrevocable. Remember how Isaac blessed his son from the depth of his heart after eating what he had requested

SECURING YOUR FUTURE

the son to bring to him. Even though it was not Esau that he told that brought it but Jacob, Isaac was still so deeply satisfied that he blessed him. There is no parent except a wicked one that will want his or her child to be a failure. Even if they have not been able to take adequate care of you because they do not have much money, provide for them that they may pray for you.

Another important thing to note in securing your future is that she was diligent. To secure your future, be diligent. The Bible says,

"Seest thou a man diligent in his business? he shall stand before kings; he shall not stand before mean men." (Proverbs 22:29, KJV)

A man that is diligent in his business, will not stand before mere men, he will stand before kings. Learn from the ant. If you work hard, you are laying the right path to securing your future. When Elisha, the man of God, told the widow to go and borrow containers, if she had been slack about it and just borrowed a few containers, she would not have been able to pay her debt. Remember in that story, it was the number of containers that she borrowed that the oil was enough for. If she had gotten more, the oil would have continued to flow. But she brought in a certain quantity and the oil stopped. Imagine if she only took one or two containers. Be diligent. You cannot be a professing Christian and be lazy, you cannot be a professing Christian and be a failure.

Finally, she was healthy and strong. When her sons brought in the oil, it was the woman who poured the oil into the vessels. It suggests she ate the right things and she was not obese nor malnourished. It is necessary to watch what you eat. Some sicknesses come with old age. When you check it out, you will find out that when people were much younger, they did not eat the right foods. Do not eat just anything. Your health future may not be secured if you eat just anything. The Bible says in 1 Corinthians 10:31 that whether you eat, or drink do all to the glory of God. Do you eat to the glory of God or do you eat just to satisfy your bodily desires? Do you fill your body with ice cream today, sweets tomorrow, soft drinks day in and day out? They are not sinful, but they are not good for your health. Check your blood pressure regularly. Go for medical check-ups. Not everyone can eat eggs every day. Some people have sugared their systems so much in times past, that the future God has for them is being weakened and redesigned by diseases such as diabetes. The Lord will deliver anyone suffering from diabetes in Jesus' name. Watch what you eat, watch what you drink.

In summary, we learn from the wife of the son of the prophets the following lessons: recognise your situation, run to God for help, be obedient to God, know how to align your speech with His word, have a good relationship with your Heavenly Father by paying your tithes/offerings/giving, have a good relationship with people around you, honour your parents, be diligent and finally watch what you eat.

Prayer

Father I receive grace to be desperate in the place of prayer until my breakthrough comes in Jesus' name. Amen.

Chapter Five

Discovering Your Buried Potentials

We have discovered from the life of Isaac, the son of Abraham, that it is possible to receive abundance from God during a famine or during an economic meltdown or during a pandemic. We have identified that he was obedient, hardworking, and persistent in the face of opposition. We have also seen from the example of the widow whose sons were to be taken away by creditors that the little jar of oil in her house, obedience, a right attitude and following divine instructions were influential in helping her secure her future, and that of her sons.

In this chapter, we wish to highlight that the Lord has a plan for every life.

"For I know the thoughts that I think toward you, saith the LORD, thoughts of peace, and not of evil, to give you an expected end." (Jeremiah 29:11, KJV)

He has deposited into each of us internal resources such as skills, potentials, abilities, talents, intelligence and much more. He has also placed around us several external resources such as people resources, technological resources, mineral resources, time, and much more. Our role is to discover His plans and

SECURING YOUR FUTURE

purposes for our lives and to deploy these internal and external resources to become the kind of person the Lord has designed us to be. Our Lord is the Maker of Heaven and Earth. He is the Grand Architect,

"All things were made by him; and without him was not anything made that was made." (John 1:3, KJV).

He can make something out of nothing. With Him all things are possible.

In Isaiah 60:15 the Bible states,

"Whereas thou hast been forsaken and hated, so that no man went through thee, I will make thee an eternal excellency, a joy of many generations." (Isaiah 60:15, KJV)

Even if we are hated as Isaac was by the Philistines, God loves us so much more. When God says He wants to make you an eternal excellency and a joy to many generations, what He needs to make that happen is already inside of you. What He needs to make you a joy to many generations is already inside of you. If it is not inside you, then he is going to look for it around you and bring it to you. What matters at the end of the day is that He is going to make you a joy to many generations and an Eternal Excellency.

He said to Abraham in Genesis 12:2,

"And I will make of thee a great nation, and I will bless thee, and make thy name great; and thou shalt be a blessing:" (Genesis 12:2, KJV)

He does not want us to be feeble or poor human beings. He wants us to be great and to be a blessing to our generation.

God has placed several things inside you and around you. Everything He needs to make you what He wants you to be is already available. He is the one who says He will make you great. In Isaiah 60:22 the Bible says,

"A little one shall become a thousand, and a small one a strong nation: I the LORD will hasten it in his time." (Isaiah 60:22, KJV)

We can see that He will increase us. He will enlarge our coast. He says a small one will become a strong nation. The seed from Abraham became a nation. That is just one man. Apply that to yourself. I do not know what level you are today. But listen to what God is telling you about your situation. Listen to your own heart. From that verse, He says a little one will become a thousand. He says a small one will become a strong nation. "I the Lord will hasten it in his time." Let us believe God for it. The seed has been placed within us waiting for us to cultivate it. In Deuteronomy 1:11,

"The LORD God of your fathers make you a thousand times so many more as ye are, and bless you, as he hath promised you" (Deuteronomy 1:11, KJV)

Our Lord God can make you a thousand times more prosperous than you are today.

I heard a prayer a few years ago that God's anointing power can do the work of ten years in one month or in one year. It means that what took others ten years to accomplish, you will accomplish it in a month or in a year. May God release such anointing upon your life in Jesus' Name. If your heart is yearning for something excessively big, unless you believe God for it, you might just be taking incremental steps when you should be taking multiplying steps. May you receive multiplying steps in Jesus' name. God wants you to excel, to be fruitful, to multiply, to live an abundant life, and to be a blessing to your generation.

He wants you to reach heaven. It is not just about here. It is also about the place that Jesus has gone to prepare for you. He says it in John chapter 14, "I go to prepare a place for you where I am, there shall you also be." God's plan for you is to make you an Eternal Excellency, to make your life beautiful, to make you a joy to many generations. The Lord Jesus Christ is a joy to many generations. Pastor E.A. Adeboye, the General Overseer of RCCG, Nelson Mandela and many others have been a joy to many generations. We thank God for their lives. You can also make such an impact that even after you leave this earth what you did would still count in Jesus' name.

Remember that we saw in the Bible that a good man leaves an inheritance even for his children's children. But this is not limited to just your biological children. When Pastor E.A. Adeboye is talking about his children, he is not only talking about his biological children. He is talking about as many as his life has impacted. There are so many people who look up to him and who thank God for his life. The impact that God wants you to have is not limited to just the biological children you have or will have. The impact He wants you to have is for many lives that you will come across, even generations yet unborn. But you must have that desire. You must desire that what God says concerning you will come to pass. What has God deposited in you? Remember Jesus said to Peter that "I will make you fishers of men."

What Peter needed to be a fisher of men was already inside of him. He did not go to the market to look for it. There are things He has already put inside of you that He wants to use to make you become what He plans for you to become.

In the parable of the talents in Matthew 25: 14-15,

"For the kingdom of heaven is as a man travelling into a far country, who called his own servants, and delivered unto them his goods. And unto one he gave five talents, to another two, and

to another one; to every man according to his several abilities; and straightway took his journey." (Matthew 25:14-15, KJV)

The Lord gives us some hints in verses 14 and 15. We see that according to every man's ability God gives, God deposits, and God puts. He does not put it there for the sake of putting. He has put it there for a reason so that there may be fruit or profit. In Genesis 15: 1-5

"After these things, the word of the LORD came unto Abram in a vision, saying, Fear not, Abram: I am thy shield, and thy exceeding great reward. And Abram said, Lord GOD, what wilt thou give me, seeing I go childless, and the steward of my house is this Eliezer of Damascus? And Abram said, Behold, to me thou hast given no seed: and, lo, one born in my house is mine heir. And behold, the word of the LORD came unto him, saying, This shall not be thine heir; but he that shall come forth out of thine own bowels shall be thine heir. And he brought him forth abroad, and said, Look now toward heaven, and tell the stars, if thou be able to number them: and he said unto him, So shall thy seed be." (Genesis 15:1-5, KJV)

Abraham assumed that he had no seed and that his servant Eliezer would be the heir to all that God had promised him. But God had deposited something in him – a son from his own loins. Abraham had already closed his own case as far as bearing children was concerned. But he did not know that from his own loins, nations would come.

Like many of us would have done, judging from physical evidence, Abraham concluded that he could not bear a child. He concluded that his servant would be his heir. That is what we often do. We accept an available alternative even though our heart yearns for something different. Abraham decided to make his servant his heir since God had not given him a son and he did not expect that it would still be possible for him to have a son. He made an alternative plan. But God said, "This one shall not be your heir, but one who will come from your own body shall be your heir." That is Abraham's own seed. That seed was already inside of him. He had it but he did not know that he had it. What do you have inside of you? Are you also thinking the way Abraham thought? Are you thinking that you do not have that which you need? The Lord has already placed in your life all that you need to become successful–talent, potential, gifts, ideas, abilities, skills, thinking faculty, creativity, you name it. The Bible says that as a man thinketh in his heart so is he. Your thinking faculty is already there. But if you do not put it to use in the right dimension, you may not get the best from it.

The Bible states in 1 John 4:4,

"Ye are of God, little children, and have overcome them: because greater is he that is in you, than he that is in the world." (1 John 4:4, KJV)

And in Psalms 71:21,

"Thou shalt increase my greatness, and comfort me on every side." (Psalms 71:21, KJV)

We have seen that God has deposited the potential for greatness in us. He has also placed other things such as talents, gifts, or capabilities in us. It is what is in you that counts. But most often what is in us is left undiscovered, undeveloped, untouched, un-deployed.

Capability is what you can do. Potential is hidden ability. Now ask yourself, "What capabilities are in me, what am I able to do that I am not doing? What are my hidden abilities and potential?"

When you discover them, make the effort to work on them. Subject them to training. Do not allow the capabilities or hidden abilities to lie there untrained. Give them a boost. It might be the ability to sing, it might be the ability to play the piano, it could be anything.

There is at least one potential in each of us that we have left untapped. For instance, this book, 'Securing Your Future' was an untapped potential inside of me. It is the result of putting together past study and teaching into a book. How much effort did it take? It took studying the Word, it took reading other books, it took going through concordances to bring out scriptures. I believed that inside of me there is the ability to write a book, I put my heart to it, I asked God for grace, and He gave me permission and directed me on how to package it. As a result, we have a book called 'Securing Your Future.'

If, you want to do anything great, you must research, and burn the midnight oil. If I get to the gates of heaven and I am asked, "Oladapo, you had thirty books inside of you, but how many did you write?" At least I can say I wrote one. Is it not better than someone who had that many and wrote nothing? You can also explore the hidden abilities in you by volunteering to serve in the house of God.

People are needed in churches to play keyboards, drums, and other musical instruments. There are potentially great singers with untrained voices. There are things God has deposited in you, waiting for you to train them, waiting for you to give them a little more push. I once read somewhere that the potential of the average person is like a large sea or ocean that no one has been able to sail on, a new continent that has not been explored, a world of possibilities waiting to be released, or an innate ability yet untapped, that cannot be seen, but can do great things. It is there. I cannot see it, but it can do great things.

Exodus 31: 2-5 says,

"See, I have called by name Bezaleel the son of Uri, the son of Hur, of the tribe of Judah: And I have filled him with the spirit of God, in wisdom, and in understanding, and in knowledge, and in all manner of workmanship, To devise cunning works, to work in gold, and in silver, and in brass, And in cutting of stones, to set

them, and in carving of timber, to work in all manner of work-manship." (Exodus 31:2-5, KJV)

God has deposited something in every one of us that we can use. That is why we have people who are artists, academics, public speakers, event managers, and etc. You therefore have a responsibility to discover, develop, and deploy all these hidden talents, potential, and gifts that the Lord has buried in you for such a time as this.

Another important thing in securing your future is to develop the potential in you. Ronaldo, a star football player, gets paid several million pounds to play football for a club. He gets paid that much to kick a ball. How much more a Christian who is operating the covenant of God. What Ronaldo has done is to train the ability that he saw in himself or that someone else saw in him. In everybody there is a seed of greatness. But something must happen for that seed to come out.

E.W. Kenyon in his book Sign Posts On The Road to Success says this,

"It is what you are, what you have in you that counts. It is the undeveloped resources in your mind, in your spirit in that inward man that counts. It is the developing of the writer, the thinker, the teacher, the inventor, the leader, the business manager that is hidden deep in you that is important. I venture that everyone of you young men and women who read this have in you one of these abilities. There may be an untrained voice, untrained musical ability lying hidden under the careless, thoughtless exterior. Let us go down with a flashlight and look over the untouched treasures that are stored away inside, that have never been touched never been used. Then let us bring the thing up that we find and make it worthwhile; give it a commercial value. For remember that everything that goes toward making you a success is inside of you. The thing that makes opportunities, that makes money, that

saves money, that creates new things that brings together things that others have created but were unable to utilise is inside of you.

Find it and make it work. It is going to require a boss who is utterly heartless to rule over you. The boss is inside of you. There is a slave driver in there whom you must bring out. Put the whip in his hand and tell him to go to it and make you a success". (Kenyon 1966, Page 13-14)

The summary of all of that is that there is something in you that would make you great if you do the necessary things.

Where do you get gold from? In the ground. Where do you get diamond from? In the ground. Where do you get crude oil? You need to drill, that is hard work. The oil is far below, equipment is needed, funds are needed, effort is needed, but if you really want to, you will get it. So you can dig it. How far do you have to dig? I do not know but unless you are determined. Whatever you need to do to get that something to come out, please do. If you need to go school, go to school. Something must come out. Why?

Because God has deposited something there. You might need to take training to bring it out, you might need to pray, to study your Bible to bring it out. You might need to fast, whatever you need to do to bring it out, do it.

Pastor E.A. Adeboye spends a lot of time in the place of prayer, the place of worship, and he spends a lot of time fasting. Unless you discipline yourself to carry out consistent spiritual and physical exercises, your life might remain the same.

Ask God to help you bring out that ability, those resources, that gift. Ask Him to teach you what you need to do. Abraham asked God, "What would you do for me seeing that I go childless. But Isaac was in his loins all the while. He had no idea that something was there. Are you also thinking like Abraham did, that

SECURING YOUR FUTURE

nothing is there? I tell you that something is there, and you must bring it out.

Pray that God will teach you what you need to do to get your hidden potential to come out. It must come out. Abraham presented the option of his servant as his heir to God. He went to God with an option that would not work. You must go back to God and ask for His own option, not your own option. Decide to do whatever it would take. Ask God to tell you what it would take. "Will it take my praying for hours daily, will it take studying the Word? Will it take me going back to school? Whatever it will take, Lord it must come out."

That ability, talent, or potential must come out. Everything you have put in me that is lying dormant must come out, Lord let them come out.

In Genesis 15:1,

"After these things, the word of the LORD came unto Abram in a vision, saying, Fear not, Abram: I am thy shield, and thy exceeding great reward." (Genesis 15:1, KJV)

The word of God came to Abram, he then asked God how His promise to him would be fulfilled since he was childless. He said one of his servants Eliezer born in his house would therefore have to be his heir.

There was a yearning, a stirring, a question, a desire within Abraham and he took it to God. A servant becoming his heir was the solution Abraham could see but God said it was not the solution. What yearning is there in your own life? What questions are burning in your heart about your future, that you want to ask God? You can go ahead and ask God. You must wait on Him until you get an answer from him. If you do not get an answer, go back to Him. It may take time for the manifestation to come but it is better to know ahead of time what answer God has to the issues of your life. If there is a yearning within you, follow the example of Abraham, ask God.

You could ask God, "You said I would be a strong nation, is it through this job that I am doing? Or how do you want me to go about it?"

Many years ago, the General Overseer of the Redeemed Christian Church of God (R.C.C.G.) was looking for people to sow a seed of $50. A well-known Pentecostal Pastor who was a minister in the RCCG then, went after the programme to see the General Overseer and offered to sow the seed and he did. At that time, this minister was trusting God for a car loan from his office to buy a car. Instead he got a letter which he thought was the approval for the loan, but it was a sack letter. Ah! He later learnt that he could not get the kind of blessing he was looking for with that type of job. There is a process God wants to use to get you to where you ought to be. That sack letter was part of what led him to start his own law chambers and things moved on from there. Go to God in prayers, ask Him questions about how His promises in your life would be fulfilled. There is a timing element, but God has said He will hasten it as He said in Jeremiah 1:12,

"Then said the LORD unto me, Thou hast well seen: for I will hasten my word to perform it." (Jeremiah 1:12, KJV)

If the Lord says stay where you are and continue, obey Him, if He says move, then do whatever He says to you.

Another important point to note is that people are links to your destiny. There are people, things, or opportunities that God has placed around you. How do we harness these links? The truth is that there are some people around you and unless that link exists, you cannot get that which they are supposed to be to you. But that link starts with you. From the account of the widow of Elisha's servant in 2 Kings 4: 1-7, the woman ran to Elisha and said that the creditors wanted to take her sons. Elisha asked her, "What do you have in your house?" She said nothing but a jar of oil. He told her to borrow vessels from her neighbours and continue to pour into the vessels, that the oil would not finish. Those neighbours have been there all along. She did not know that they would someday be the links by which she would get out of debt by lending her their vessels.

Your fellow church members or your colleagues could be the link by which a miracle would happen in your life.

Just imagine if that widow had been treating her neighbours badly. Then in her time of need, she went knocking at their door to borrow their vessels. They could have said, "I don't have any container, or I am using the container. Always remember that apart from the fact that God has deposited some things in us for greatness, He has placed several people and things around us to serve as the link to our destiny. Unless there is a yearning within you, you may never establish this connection. It was when she ran to the man of God, and he gave her an instruction and she had to follow the instruction that she used the relationship links with her neighbours. Those links had always been there.

Thank God she had been living a good life, and she was able to go to them and borrow several containers. I believe she must have been a good neighbour. People around us are links to help us bring out what we already have with us or in us and what we have in us is what counts. It was somebody that introduced and linked Joseph to Pharaoh that helped him interpret Pharaoh's dreams. That single interpretation for Pharaoh paved the way for Joseph to become the second ruler in the land. He moved from a prisoner to become the Prime Minister. It was someone that linked and introduced David to play the instrument for Saul so that the evil spirit would depart from him. It was that music talent that brought him to stay in the palace. Place a high value on all your relationships as you do not know which one of them will link you to your next miracle.

Prayers

Father open my eyes to see all the potential that you have deposited in my life and help me to value all my relationships in Jesus' name. Amen.

Chapter Six

Discovering The Resources Around You

In the previous chapters, the emphasis was on the fact that the Master Planner, the Creator of the Heavens and the Earth, the Potter has a plan for your life. To secure your future, there is a journey that He wants you to undertake and there is a level of success that He wants you to attain. He has deposited in you: talents, potential, gifts, ideas, and skills. You are required to develop these resources. You are required to extract the treasures that He has placed inside of you. If you choose not to, nobody would do it for you. The resources of God in you will rot and remain in you as unused potential. You are also required to utilise the infinite amount of resources He has placed around you. Jeremiah 29:11 says,

"For I know the thoughts that I think toward you, saith the LORD, thoughts of peace, and not of evil, to give you an expected end." (Jeremiah 29:11, KJV)

Everything He needs to multiply you is already inside of you. Unless you do the necessary things to bring out your gifts and talents, they will remain there.

Newton's first law of motion states that everything continues in a state of uniform rest or motion unless an external force act on it. This means that an object will remain in a position until someone or something moves it. Crude oil remains in the ground until it is drilled. The same holds for your potential. You must do something. As Christians, you should ask, "Lord, what would You have me do? What is it that You have placed in me?"

We have also seen that apart from the fact that God has placed things inside of us, He has also placed a lot of things around us. All around us He has strategically placed people, his Word, assets, and opportunities. It is only when we open our eyes, or He opens our eyes that we can see them. In Genesis 13:14-18 the Bible says,

"And the LORD said unto Abram, after that Lot was separated from him, Lift up now thine eyes, and look from the place where thou art northward, and southward, and eastward, and west-ward: For all the land which thou seest, to thee will I give it, and to thy seed for ever. And I will make thy seed as the dust of the earth: so that if a man can number the dust of the earth, then shall thy seed also be numbered. Arise, walk through the land in the length of it and in the breadth of it; for I will give it unto thee. Then Abram removed his tent, and came and dwelt in the plain of Mamre, which is in Hebron, and built there an altar unto the LORD." (Genesis 13:14-18, KJV)

The Lord asked Abraham to lift his eyes to look around from the position where he was standing to see the land that was before him. You need to intentionally look around you and see the opportunities that are around you so that you can possess them. There are many things the Lord has placed around us that are stepping-stones to secure our future. Until you see them, you cannot possess them.

Exodus 4: 1- 5 says,

"And Moses answered and said, But, behold, they will not believe me, nor hearken unto my voice: for they will say, The LORD hath not appeared unto thee. And the LORD said unto him, what is that in thine hand? And he said, A rod. And he said, Cast it on the ground. And he cast it on the ground, and it became a serpent; and Moses fled from before it. And the LORD said unto Moses, put forth thine hand, and take it by the tail. And he put forth his hand, and caught it, and it became a rod in his hand: That they may believe that the LORD God of their fathers, the God of Abraham, the God of Isaac, and the God of Jacob, hath appeared unto thee. And the LORD said furthermore unto him, Put now thine hand into thy bosom." (Exodus 4:1-5, KJV)

The rod in the hand of Moses was so ordinary until the Lord asked him to throw it down and it became a serpent. What are the things around you today that you consider as ordinary? Who are the people around you that you despise or ignore? Do you remember Naaman's servant girl? She was just a slave. But it was this slave who showed him the way for deliverance from his leprosy. You may think some things or people you have around you are ordinary, but God has strategically placed them around you.

Let us read Genesis 21:14-19,

"And Abraham rose up early in the morning, and took bread, and a bottle of water, and gave it unto Hagar, putting it on her shoulder, and the child, and sent her away: and she departed, and wandered in the wilderness of Beersheba. And the water was spent in the bottle, and she cast the child under one of the shrubs. And she went, and sat her down over against him a good way off, as it were a bowshot: for she said, Let me not see the death of the child. And she sat over against him, and lift up her voice, and wept. And God heard the voice of the lad; and the angel of God called to Hagar out of heaven, and said unto her, What aileth thee, Hagar?

fear not; for God hath heard the voice of the lad where he is. Arise, lift up the lad, and hold him in thine hand; for I will make him a great nation. And God opened her eyes, and she saw a well of water; and she went, and filled the bottle with water, and gave the lad drink." (Genesis 21:14-19, KJV)

Abraham had asked Hagar to leave with her child. The water he gave her had finished. Her baby was crying, and she was crying as well. She put him under a shrub so that she would not see him die. You may be jumping up and down like Hagar and crying. She was anxious, she was afraid. But God said, "Fear not, open your eyes." Then she saw the well and I ask myself. Did the well just spring up? Or was it there before? The well had always been there. The solution to that challenge whether it is financial, spiritual, physical, whatever you may be going through, is already around you. It has always been there. The Lord has placed it there already, but your eyes have to be opened. Remember he said to Abraham, "Lift up your eyes." He said to Hagar, "Open your eyes." Unless your eyes are opened, you may be looking but not seeing. May you see in Jesus' name. Amen.

if it had been a river, Hagar might have seen it because it is probably what she was looking out for. And if it had been a river there would probably have been other people fetching water, so she would not have missed it. Many of us are always on the lookout for the big thing that everyone else is already doing, not the seemingly small things like the well that no one else had noticed. If we listen to God, we will know what God wants us to do and if we take one step at a time, it will grow, and we will enjoy it before other people notice it. Examples abound of people that started businesses with only an exceedingly small amount of money and today they are extraordinarily successful.

Let us reflect again on the story of the widow, whose husband was one of the sons of the prophet in 2 Kings Chapter 4. She did not have to buy anything before running to see the man of God. The man of God she ran to had always been there. The little oil

DISCOVERING THE RESOURCES AROUND YOU

that she had left was always there. The sons that helped her were already there. The neighbours that she ran to had always been there. But when she ran to the man of God, he connected her to her success by giving her instructions to use what she already had, and she obeyed.

God has placed His word within our reach to read, to study, to listen, to speak. There are so many treasures that God has placed for us to find and do in His word. When we follow these instructions, as the widow followed the man of God's instructions, we will get tangible results as she did.

Thy words were found, and I did eat them; and thy word was unto me the joy and rejoicing of mine heart: for I am called by thy name, O LORD God of hosts." (Jeremiah 15:16, KJV)

Our responsibility is to read, to discover, to obtain inspiration and insights from the Word of God, and to follow the instruction. Thereafter, leave the rest to God.

Some years ago, before I got married, I needed to pay my rent. The landlord had given me the reminder letter to pay up my annual rent. I remembered that I had always been told that as a Christian you should not get to the point where you really need something without the provision being already there. Your eyes may not see it, but the provision is available. I believed there was provision. I recalled from the Scriptures the story of the widow woman with the little jar of oil. The oil had always been there even when the creditors came to threaten to take away her sons.

I began asking questions in the place of prayer to know how to access the provision that I believed God had already made available for me to pay my rent. As we have been taught when you do not know what to pray about, pray in tongues. When you pray in tongues you speak mysteries to God.

"For he that speaketh in an unknown tongue speaketh not unto men, but unto God: for no man understandeth him; howbeit in the spirit he speaketh mysteries." (1 Corinthians 14:2, KJV)

I started to pray in tongues. As I was praying, I believed that what I needed to pay the rent was already available even though I could not see it. I was wondering whether I needed to sell my air conditioning unit or my deep freezer or my armchairs to access the provision.

As I was praying, my eyes fell on a polythene bag that a friend of mine had brought to me earlier on that month. The bag had commercial pamphlets to market satellite dishes for watching satellite television. This was before cable TV. I was supposed to look for potential customers to market the satellite dishes for him.

I went to the bag and brought out the pamphlets and began to pray again, asking in my spirit, "Who should I go to?"

The Holy Spirit ministered to me to ask my neighbour, a businessman, to enquire whether he would be interested in buying a satellite dish. Almost immediately the power went out. This happened in the evening, at about 6pm. The Holy Spirit told me, "Your neighbour will go downstairs now that the power has been cut. Dress up, go down and wait for him downstairs with the pamphlet in your hand." I obeyed and truly, he came downstairs. We used to call him Chairman in those days.

"Chairman! I sell Satellite dishes," I told him. "Really!' he said, "I've been searching for a Satellite dish to buy." he said. That was how Chairman agreed to buy a satellite dish from me and he actually bought the dish. I made my own profit and paid my rent. Chairman had always been there. The pamphlets had been there in my sitting room for over two weeks before I had the burden to search in the place of prayer about how to pay my rent.

DISCOVERING THE RESOURCES AROUND YOU

God will not leave you empty handed. The Bible says in Psalm 37:25,

"I have been young, and now am old; yet have I not seen the righteous forsaken, nor his seed begging bread." (Psalms 37:25, KJV)

He has placed certain things around us but most of the time, our eyes are closed. One of those things is His word. His word never fails. Remember Elijah during the famine in 1 Kings 17, if he had despised God's word, he would not have gone to the brook and he would not have been fed by a raven day and night. When the brook he drank water from dried up, another instruction came. The Bible says,

"And the word of the LORD came unto him, saying, Arise, get thee to Zarephath, which belongeth to Zidon, and dwell there: behold, I have commanded a widow woman there to sustain thee." (1 Kings 17:8-9, KJV)

The word of the Lord came to Elijah and gave him a fresh set of instructions for his provision. God always makes a way. You will not spend the last money on you in Jesus' name.

Many years ago, Bishop Oyedepo shared the story about the time he and his wife had to ration their resources because of scarcity in the land. His wife said, "Be careful of that soap because that's the last soap in the house." And he said to her, "That CANNOT be the last soap in the house." That came out of the revelation that the God he served is a provider and will always make a way of provision.

There was another time that we had a problem with the use of our church auditorium. The authorities had locked up the church auditorium and premises as they wanted to prevent us from using the place. However, they left the pedestrian gate open. As I read the Bible, the scripture in Nehemiah 4:14 stood out,

"And I looked, and rose up, and said unto the nobles, and to the rulers, and to the rest of the people, Be not ye afraid of them: remember the Lord, which is great and terrible, and fight for your brethren, your sons, and your daughters, your wives, and your houses." (Nehemiah 4:14, KJV)

I took that as an instruction from God, so I decided we were going to use the compound for our church service the following day.

Some people tried to restrain me because they were afraid of the authorities. But I had no fear. The only concern I had was that people close to me said on Saturday night, "I don't think we should have service in the church compound." They almost put fear in me. But I remembered what Jesus said when He told Peter, "Get thee behind me." The same Peter, who had said something borne out of divine revelation to Jesus earlier was the same person that spoke discouraging words to Jesus a little later. Even though they said, "I don't think we should do that," I was clear that God had told me to have service in the church compound and I remembered His word, 'Be ye not afraid of them.'

What I am saying is that when you have a Word from the Lord, it will come to pass because with God all things are possible. We should always find out what God is saying concerning any situation we are in. If God has told you, the issue is settled. There might be challenges but He will take care of them. But if God did not tell you and you go ahead, anything can happen.

Frustration comes when you are standing on a word that God did not give you. When it does not come to pass, frustration sets in. But, when God gives you a word and you are holding on to that word, you are not moved by the situation. In a previous chapter, we saw how God told Isaac to stay in a place even though there was famine. Isaac did and he prospered, although challenges came, he overcame every one of them. All your detractors will leave you alone and the word of God will be fulfilled in your life.

Prayers

Father open my eyes to see all the resources that you have placed around me for my success in Jesus' name. Amen.

Chapter Seven

Choosing To Be Rich

The person who secures his future in Christ Jesus has chosen to be rich by using the resources placed in and around him as his access to prosperity. No matter what your circumstances are today, prosperity is still possible. As stated in Deuteronomy 8:18,

"But thou shalt remember the LORD thy God: for it is he that giveth thee power to get wealth, that he may establish his covenant which he sware unto thy fathers, as it is this day." (Deuteronomy 8:18, KJV)

It is God that gives us power to get wealth that His covenant might be established. In addition, the Bible states in 3 John 1:2,

"Beloved, I wish above all things that thou mayest prosper and be in health, even as thy soul prospereth." (3 John 1:2, KJV)

The plan and purpose of God for us is that as our soul prospers, He will prosper the work of our hands and keep us healthy. Furthermore, the Bible states in Isaiah 48:17,

"Thus saith the LORD, thy Redeemer, the Holy One of Israel; I am the LORD thy God which teacheth thee to profit, which leadeth thee by the way that thou shouldest go." (Isaiah 48:17, KJV)

The Lord is ready to teach us and to lead us along the path of prosperity. May the testimony of God concerning Jacob in Genesis 30:43 be your testimony.

"And the man increased exceedingly, and had much cattle, and maidservants, and menservants, and camels, and asses." (Genesis 30:43, KJV)

Possibility can be defined as something that can be done, something that can exist, something that can be achieved or something that can happen. The word possibility means potential progress. A living dog is better than a dead lion. The possibility of the Christian life is that God can take you from where you are in the dung hill today and place you in the palace tomorrow.

"For with God nothing shall be impossible." (Luke 1:37, KJV)

Anything is possible with God. Joseph's life is an exceptionally good example. Even though Joseph had dreamt of being a ruler over his family he suddenly found himself as a slave in the house of Potiphar. Possibilities emerge when you have a dream, an idea, or a belief that your circumstances can change. Possibilities make you realise that it is possible that you can make it in life against all odds, that it is possible that you can be promoted, that it is possible that this business deal can come to pass.

Everything you see today started as an idea. The Bible says that,

"In the beginning God created the heaven and the earth." (Genesis 1:1, KJV)

God is a creator and we were created in His image as shown in Genesis Chapter 1.

"And God said, Let us make man in our image, after our likeness: and let them have dominion over the fish of the sea, and over the fowl of the air, and over the cattle, and over all the earth, and over every creeping thing that creepeth upon the earth. So, God created man in his own image, in the image of God created he him; male and female created he them." (Genesis 1:26-27, KJV)

Therefore, the Lord has deposited creative abilities into you and I, so that we can continue the work of creating things. For instance, God created trees, but He did not create the chair. However, He put within man the ability to create the chair. He put crude oil in the ground. The plastic chair is a derivative of crude oil. But God did not create the plastic chair. It came as an idea to someone, a possibility. The person worked on the possibility and today, we have plastic chairs of different colours.

God created the cotton plant that grows. But today man uses cotton to make clothes. Remember, Adam and Eve did not have clothes. It was after they sinned that they cut leaves to cover themselves, but the Lord had put cotton there as a plant. The possibilities had been put there but it did not materialise until it came as an idea, a thought, a dream, or a possibility to someone.

Every dream or idea you have has the ability to come to pass. Energy saving light is now a reality but even some years ago we did not have that. But somebody must have been concerned that we are consuming so much electricity and wondered if it would be possible to create the same light in such a way that it would not consume so much energy. It started as an idea, a need that needed to be met, something that needed to be satisfied. Because of that need, some people conducted research and came up with an idea.

The world is waiting for the product that you and I will bring to pass because God has placed in us potential, talents, skills, gifts, and abilities. No one was created empty. God has placed in us so much godly deposit to enable us to accomplish great things for

Securing Your Future

Him. Unfortunately, most of us have fallen far below expectation. God has also placed resources around us. Such resources include people that he has placed around us and His words and generally things that could be useful to us.

Remember the woman in 1 Kings 4: 1-7. Prophet Elisha said, "Go and borrow pots from your neighbours." So, she ran to collect pots. The neighbours had been there all along. There are people around you today in your office, in church, where you live, that God has placed certain things in their lives that He will use for your miracle and breakthrough. Unless you open your eyes, even though those people are there, and the things are there, nothing would happen.

Many people have opportunities staring them in the face but unfortunately, they are unable to see them.

For anyone who wants to prosper financially, there are other streams of income apart from your current business or job. Though Nigerians are complaining about the lack of opportunities, do you know that the number of foreigners coming in to invest and to work in Nigeria continues to increase?

Why are they here? It is because there is still a lot to go round and reach everybody in this country. There are still a lot of money-making opportunities in this country. Foreigners are leaving their own countries to come here to make money. Meanwhile, people here are seeking ways to check out and to go and work in mortuaries to earn money in order to survive in England or the USA. The foreigners that are coming here in large numbers to invest have seen the opportunities, the potential, and the possibilities. It must be that their eyes are opened, and our own eyes are closed. May your eyes be opened in Jesus' name. Amen.

When God opens your eyes, you will be able to generate a business idea that would fulfil a need or a demand that will make you to earn income. There must be a product that you can sell

CHOOSING TO BE RICH

and there must be somebody willing to buy it. You must have a way to sell it.

Let us learn some lessons from the man called Jacob in the Bible. Much has been said about Jacob, that he is a trickster, a deceiver and so on. But the Bible also repeatedly says the God of Abraham, the God of Isaac, and the God of Jacob. This suggests that in the scheme of things God recognised Jacob as a covenant descendant of Abraham. What caught my attention was that twenty-four chapters, from Genesis 25 to Genesis 49, were focused on the life of Jacob and his family. It means that Jacob was not just an ordinary person. For the Bible to devote so many chapters to his life, it means that we are supposed to learn some lessons from his life.

"And Isaac intreated the LORD for his wife, because she was barren: and the LORD was intreated of him, and Rebekah his wife conceived. And the children struggled together within her; and she said, If it be so, why am I thus? And she went to enquire of the LORD. And the LORD said unto her, Two nations are in thy womb, and two manner of people shall be separated from thy bowels; and the one people shall be stronger than the other people; and the elder shall serve the younger. And when her days to be delivered were fulfilled, behold, there were twins in her womb. And the first came out red, all over like an hairy garment; and they called his name Esau. And after that came his brother out, and his hand took hold on Esau's heel; and his name was called Jacob: and Isaac was threescore years old when she bare them. And the boys grew: and Esau was a cunning hunter, a man of the field; and Jacob was a plain man, dwelling in tents. And Isaac loved Esau because he did eat of his venison: but Rebekah loved Jacob. And Jacob sod pottage: and Esau came from the field, and he was faint: And Esau said to Jacob, Feed me, I pray thee, with that same red pottage; for I am faint: therefore was his name called Edom. And Jacob said, Sell me this day thy birth right. And Esau said, Behold, I am at the point to die: and what profit shall this birth right do to me? And Jacob said, Swear to me this day; and he sware unto him: and he sold his birthright unto Jacob. Then Jacob gave Esau bread and pottage of

SECURING YOUR FUTURE

lentiles; and he did eat and drink, and rose up, and went his way: thus Esau despised his birthright." (Genesis 25:21-34, KJV)

Verse 27 reveals that Esau was a cunning hunter, a man of the fields, and Jacob was a plain man dwelling in tents. Esau goes to the field to hunt. You will find out that hunters use up a lot of energy running after game such as antelopes as they work to outsmart the animal, before eventually succeeding in killing it and carrying it home. That is the kind of work Esau was doing.

One day he came back home tired and hungry. The Bible tells us Jacob was skilled in cooking. What skill do you have? What are you using it for? Jacob used what he had to get something very precious–the birthright which made the first born entitled to the family wealth, in this case the blessings of God. Jacob had a cooking skill and his brother had a need; he was hungry. There was a deal. Jacob said, "I give you food, you give me your birthright." The food was appetising enough for Esau to agree.

There are many people who can cook but have not used that skill. I have heard that in Lagos today we have over 20 million people. Those that work in the fast food industry understand the kind of skill that Jacob had. Many families can cook but they still buy food from restaurants like Sweet Sensations, Mr Biggs, Tasty Fried Chicken and etc. Every day, people exchange what they have for what they do not have. You can just position yourself to serve about 100,000 people out of the 20 million. If you make $0.5 profit selling one meal to each of those people in a month, that is about $50,000.

Some people know how to sing well. What did Michael Jackson have? He had the skill of dancing and singing. We know the kind of money he made. He may still be alive today if he lived his life for God.

Have you heard about Ali Baba the comedian? Can jokes be learnt? Yes. Go to jokes.com on the internet, read jokes that are written there and cram them. Start by asking for the opportunity to hold the microphone at any relative's wedding. Release the jokes that you have crammed, and people will laugh and remember you. The next person that wants to plan a wedding will call you.

We all have something extraordinary that we can do to make money. I have a Pastor friend who had difficulty feeding his family because his business was not yielding enough money. He loves reading books. He made a firm decision. He told his wife he no longer wanted the television to be in their bedroom. He said, "I want to use the time I spend in watching TV to read motivational and success books." He began to read widely. Then he said, "I am a Pastor. God has given me the ability to talk." He had to ask himself, who do I want to talk to? And he said, I will talk to children in primary schools as well as to their teachers. They need guidance and counselling. In fact, this is the season." At the end of the school year, many schools started calling him to speak at their prize giving day ceremony. He went from school to school with the same message. For each message he was given an honorarium. He has a mouth and he can speak so he kept training himself on how he could speak better. His target audience were students and teachers and he grew from there. That is a skill! Do you have a skill? What have you done with it? May the Lord help you to discover and to deploy that skill in Jesus' name. Prosperity is possible. You must use what you have, to get what you want.

Prayers

Father help me to upgrade my skills so that my prosperity will begin to manifest in Jesus' name. Amen.

Chapter Eight

Deploying Your God Given Skills

When you identify the deposit of God in your life, you will need to refine and sharpen it until it becomes a skill that can be deployed in various situations to secure a glorious future for you. In the previous chapter we saw Jacob using the deposit of God within him, his cooking skills, to secure the birthright from his brother. In this chapter we continue to look at the life of Jacob and how he used other acquired skills and personal attributes to become great.

Genesis 27:1-8 says,

"And it came to pass, that when Isaac was old, and his eyes were dim, so that he could not see, he called Esau his eldest son, and said unto him, My son: and he said unto him, Behold, here am I. And he said, Behold now, I am old, I know not the day of my death: Now therefore take, I pray thee, thy weapons, thy quiver and thy bow, and go out to the field, and take me some venison; And make me savoury meat, such as I love, and bring it to me, that I may eat; that my soul may bless thee before I die. And Rebekah heard when Isaac spake to Esau his son. And Esau went to the field to hunt for venison, and to bring it. And Rebekah spake unto Jacob her son, saying, Behold, I heard thy father speak unto Esau thy brother, saying, Bring me venison, and make me savoury meat,

that I may eat, and bless thee before the LORD before my death. Now therefore, my son, obey my voice according to that which I command thee." (Genesis 27:1-8, KJV)

Apart from cooking skills, Jacob had relationship skills. He had a good relationship with his mother. He was not there when his father asked Esau to bring venison. His mother was not there either, but she overheard the conversation and she began to plan strategically. She said, "Son, come let me tell you something. Do what I say."

That was family politics. We have family politics, church politics, boardroom politics, government politics, and business politics. Some people are in positions that help them predict or know what is about to happen. If you have good relationship skills, these kinds of people could call you to tell you. That is what happened in Jacob's case. But with the way some people behave, nobody will tell them when there is a good opportunity. It could be that you relate with people in an offensive, harsh, or hurtful way. If you do not relate well with people, it could cause you to miss out in life.

Jacob obviously had a good relationship with his mother. If you behave nastily towards your superiors in the office, remember that at the meetings to deliberate who should be promoted, the bosses are there, and you may not be there. If a few people are to be promoted and so many are qualified, one of the bosses can call you aside and say, "If you do this and this, your promotion will be certain."

You do not need to pay money to have a good relationship with your brother, boss, subordinate, servant, neighbour, and colleagues in the office. Naaman's servant must have been treated well. That was the reason she spoke up when she saw her boss was a leper and revealed to his wife that there was a prophet in Israel through whom he could get his healing. If they had been maltreating her, would she have given him that solution? I think not. People above and below us can show us the way.

Let us go back to our text in Genesis 27:18-29. When Jacob's mother came up with the idea that he should represent his brother, he said to his mother, "You know that my brother is hairy. My father may feel me and know that I have deceived him. What am I going to do?" Jacob was not ready to go on with the plan. But his mother said, "Don't worry. Just do what I say. Bring this one, I will cook it and you will wear something on your body."

The point we should note here is that Jacob was a risk taker. Even though his mother assured him, his father could still have asked him a question that would have made it obvious that he was not Esau. His father touched him. He suspected that it was not Esau. He asked how he was able to bring the food so fast and wanted to know if it was really Esau. But his father was not seeing like he used to see before. He felt him and said he should come nearer, and he did, and he smelt his body and was satisfied.

Jacob took a risk. Anything could have happened. Are you willing to take risks? A businessman must be willing to take risks. He should not be a gambler but, he should be a risk taker. We have discussed the slothful man in Proverbs 26. The slothful man says that there is a lion outside. He has not seen the lion, but he believes there is a lion outside and so, he stays indoors and does not move.

That is the kind of man that if you ask, "What about your business?' he would say, 'the economy is bad." He comes up with a lot of excuses. Those excuses are worthless, and they simply mean that the person is not ready to take a risk. If you do not take a step forward, you will remain as you are. If a basket is placed in a position and no one moves it, in the next ten years it will remain in the same position. Unless you act, you will

SECURING YOUR FUTURE

remain where you are, suffering and smiling. Unless you act, decide, take a risk, and step out of your comfort zone, you will remain where you are.

Jacob was also recorded to be a faithful man. He was committed to whatever he says. He paid his tithe faithfully. The Bible says in Genesis 28:20-22,

"And Jacob vowed a vow, saying, If God will be with me, and will keep me in this way that I go, and will give me bread to eat, and raiment to put on, So that I come again to my father's house in peace; then shall the LORD be my God: And this stone, which I have set for a pillar, shall be God's house: and of all that thou shalt give me I will surely give the tenth unto thee." (Genesis 28:20-22, KJV)

Jacob had left his parents' house by following his mother's advice to marry from another land. On his journey, he got to a place called Bethel and slept there. In his dream, he saw angels ascending and descending from Heaven. And he said, "God must be here." And he put some stones and said, "Lord, if you will be with me in my coming and going, I am going to pay my tithes. Of all that you give me, I will give you a tenth."

He did not eat his tithes. There is a blessing that comes with payment of tithes. Bishop Oyedepo gave the testimony some years ago of a man who said to God, "Lord, this year I want to pay $3000 in tithes." What was he telling God? "For me to pay this kind of tithe, you are going to increase me like this". What I paid last year is not what I want to pay this year, I want to pay more. I have been paying tithes of $100, Lord this year I want to pay $500 or $5000 more.

Some people are paying tithes of $10,000. Do not think it is impossible for you to get to that level. Ask yourself, "What do I need to do so I can pay tithes of $10,000?"

Jacob continued and said to God, "If I can come again to my father's house in peace, then shall the Lord be my God and these stones which I have set for a pillar, shall be God's house and of all that thou shall give me I shall give a tenth." What he was saying is simply "I am going to be faithful." Many of us are not faithful in the payment of our tithes. And we want the blessings, favour and support or backing of God.

A lady came to my office for prayer some time ago. She had given someone some money for rent payment and the person ran away. When I prayed, it was laid in my heart to ask her, "Sister, do you pay your tithes?" And she said, "Ah!" She said she had no income. I asked, "Did you pay tithe on the money that this person stole?" And, she said, "No." Why won't the devourer come? God says, "And I will rebuke the devourer for your sakes." That is a promise that comes with the payment of tithes. When you do not pay tithe, the devourer can come in the morning, afternoon, or night in various ways. He comes with sickness, car breakdown, rent increases, loss of money, in various ways. As a covenant child, you have a covenant with God, you should go to him with your income and say, "Lord, take of the income you gave me."

I was once told that the owner of the company that produces a branded toothpaste was paying 90 percent of his income as tithes. He was a Christian. A lot of us use branded toothpaste. The world is waiting for your own product and my own product. Your life does not have to remain as it is, but there are spiritual principles you need to activate. If you do not activate these principles, your life remains as it is. Go back to God and state your commitment on this issue.

A man of God said he asked God, "You said You will open the windows of heaven and pour out a blessing such that there will not be room enough to receive it. What exactly are You pouring out?" God ministered to him that what He sends out are revelations, ideas, and inspiration. A revelation, idea or inspiration

SECURING YOUR FUTURE

about a business or a thing can change a man's life. The revelation Joseph had about Pharaoh's dream changed his entire life in a matter of hours. He rose from being a slave to a Prime minister of the greatest empire at that time. When you pay tithes, God gives you inspiration, ideas, and revelations that have the potential to change your life.

For many of us who pay tithes, there are potentials of greatness that are waiting for us that our eyes are not yet opened to. For those who do not pay tithes, their doors are closed but, for those who pay tithes, doors are opened. If your eyes are not opened to the ideas that God has given you, or you are not acting on them, they remain as they are. Jacob acted. We are going to see what he did with the ideas that God gave him later. Jacob had four attributes: cooking skills, relationship skills, risk taking ability, and a commitment to paying his tithes.

In Genesis chapter 30 the story of Jacob continues.

"Give me my wives and my children, for whom I have served thee, and let me go: for thou knowest my service which I have done thee. And Laban said unto him, I pray thee, if I have found favour in thine eyes, tarry: for I have learned by experience that the LORD hath blessed me for thy sake. And he said, Appoint me thy wages, and I will give it. And he said unto him, Thou knowest how I have served thee, and how thy cattle was with me. For it was little which thou hadst before I came, and it is now increased unto a multitude; and the LORD hath blessed thee since my coming: and now when shall I provide for mine own house also? And he said, What shall I give thee? And Jacob said, Thou shalt not give me any thing: if thou wilt do this thing for me, I will again feed and keep thy flock:"(Genesis 30:26-31, KJV)

Jacob had been labouring with Laban for years. He wanted to marry Laban's youngest daughter, Rachel. He laboured for seven years and Laban gave him Leah, her elder sister, to be his wife. Jacob had to labour for another seven years before he

DEPLOYING YOUR GOD GIVEN SKILLS

could marry Rachel. By this point in time, Jacob told Laban to let him go with his wives and the children. Laban knew that God had blessed him because of Jacob. Don't you wish that is your story, that things are changing for the better because you are in a place, whether it's your office, a church, or your home? That was the grace of God that was upon the life of Jacob.

We also saw that grace upon the life of his son, Joseph. Potiphar, who was Joseph's master while he was a slave, had that experience as his household was blessed because of Joseph.

It was as a result of what Jacob did that Laban said to Jacob, "Tell me what you want?" And Jacob said, "I am ready to serve with you again but, these are the terms of the contract."

Let us have a closer look again at the life of Jacob. Jacob was described as a plain man living in tents. He was a shepherd boy. His brother was a hunter who ran after animals and killed them, brought them back, but after that, did nothing. But Jacob was a cultivator. He would work with a ram and they would give birth to children. He was a cultivator so whatever he did, there was always increase and increase. While his brother Esau was killing, Jacob was cultivating and increasing.

Cultivating was another skill Jacob had which he used while working for Laban.

"I will pass through all thy flock to day, removing from thence all the speckled and spotted cattle, and all the brown cattle among the sheep, and the spotted and speckled among the goats: and of such shall be my hire. So shall my righteousness answer for me in time to come, when it shall come for my hire before thy face: every one that is not speckled and spotted among the goats, and brown among the sheep, that shall be counted stolen with me. And Laban said, Behold, I would it might be according to thy word. And he removed that day the he goats that were ringstraked and spotted, and all the she goats that were speckled and spotted, and

SECURING YOUR FUTURE

every one that had some white in it, and all the brown among the sheep, and gave them into the hand of his sons. And he set three days' journey betwixt himself and Jacob: and Jacob fed the rest of Laban's flocks." (Genesis 30:32-36, KJV)

He said to Laban, my wages would be the freckled or spotted animals. Laban took away all the animals with freckles or spots and left the ones that did not have any freckles. He did not expect the animals that did not have freckles or spots to give birth to those that would be freckled or spotted. He did not want Jacob to have any wages. But Jacob had a divine idea. He cut some trees and placed them where the cattle came to drink water and when he saw the strong ones were mating, he would put his contraption in front of them. They would see something. I do not know what they were seeing but when they gave birth, their offspring were freckled even though the parents had no freckles. When the weak ones came to mate, he would take away his contraption and kept it, so his herd of cattle increased. All the freckled and spotted cattle were strong, and they were his based on the agreement he had with Laban.

The sons of Laban were also shepherds, but they did not have the wisdom that Jacob had. Laban himself was also a shepherd, but did not have that wisdom either. What did Jacob have? I do not know, but what I do know was that Jacob paid his tithes and he was a cultivator. He had a skill different from the skills of other people, and God had given him a divine idea which he used to the maximum. He was not lazy.

"The slothful man roasteth not that which he took in hunting: but the substance of a diligent man is precious." (Proverbs 12:27, KJV)

Esau goes and hunts, but he does not roast what he hunts. So, he brings his catch back home and then somebody else cooks it for him. Roasting is a process that comes after you have killed an animal. You process it, and you cook it or whatever, and then

DEPLOYING YOUR GOD GIVEN SKILLS

it has value. By processing, you increase the value of that which was killed in hunting. But, when you kill something that you hunt and you do not process it, it will soon get rotten.

As a result, the person is desperate to sell it quickly, so that somebody else can roast it. Unless you develop your skill, you will find yourself paying much higher for something you originally developed. That is the reason the countries that know how to process crude oil are commanding much more money than countries that do not process crude oil.

What does processing mean to an individual? It means if you are skilled in singing, writing, cooking or more, you should ask yourself, "What do I need to do to make sure that this skill is not a raw skill, a village skill? How can I make it commercially viable? If I know how to talk, what do I need to do to get commercial value from this talking? Then, you have to take concrete steps to transform the skill into a skill that has commercial value.

Jacob was also a trader. He had many skills: cooking, risk-taking, paying his tithes, cultivating, or processing, and he also had the ability to trade. When he was returning home with his family, he heard that his brother Esau was coming with 400 men. Jacob offered him some of his property so that his brother would not kill him. "Give and it shall be given unto you, pressed down, shaken together and running over shall men give unto your bosom." There is something you have that if you give it out, it will open possibilities for you.

The Bible says that the gift of a man maketh room for him. The gift of a man does make room for him! Your gift will make room for you in the mighty name of Jesus. However, you must have a trader mentality. You must trade what you have in order to acquire what you want. If it is so with men, how much more with God? He will bring abundance your way if you are ready to give Him what you have.

What skill do you have? What are you ready to give up so that you can move forward? The man we spoke about earlier gave up watching television. Some people have gone back to school to learn so that they might move forward in life. What are you willing to learn?

I once read the story of a lawyer. She had gone through law school and had worked for nine months. But she went on to learn how to sew. Today, she calls herself a tailor. The income that she earns is much higher than what she used to earn as a lawyer. She gave up practicing law so that she could become a tailor.

What skills do you have? Are they lying dormant? Is your life like the man who had the one talent and buried it? What do you want to do with what you have? Will your life remain the same or will you begin to act now? Begin to ask God about the actions you need to take. To secure your future you must know and harness your skills. Those skills will make you great.

Prayer

Father let every skill, potential, ability, talent, and deposit in me begin to produce fruitful results in Jesus' name. Amen.

Chapter Nine

Harnessing The Possibilities Of The Mind

We must always keep in mind that if the woman Elisha told to go and borrow vessels had not stepped out, the neighbours would not have known that she needed vessels. It is when you step out that you would discover how close the help you need is.

When our church auditorium was closed by the government authorities, many of the workers prayed. One of our prayers was that God should send help. While we were wondering how we were going to start the service on a Sunday morning, I found out that one of our church members had called the phone number of one of those people that had been involved in shutting down the church building. This lady had the phone numbers of many people in key places on her phone. This lady had always been in our church and we did not know that she was so highly connected. We needed to write to the Executive Governor of Lagos state to complain about the church closure. We discovered that we had people within our church congregation who were close to the Executive Governor. We had to meet with top government officials and discovered that some of our church members had access to their phone numbers and were well acquainted with them. If we had not taken a step of faith, or if we did not have that problem, I would not have known that people within our church had these connections.

You would be surprised to find out that God has already placed the people and all the things you need to succeed in life around you. Unless your eyes are opened, unless you are following the leading of the Holy Spirit, you would just be there, and nothing would happen.

What must a believer do to see the kind of results experienced by Abraham, Isaac, and Jacob? The believer needs to pray for illumination, understanding of God's plan, wisdom, strength, and faith and then act. To be able to do all of these, you need to harness your mind so that it can work and make a place for you. It is from the renewed mind that we first begin to discover what is possible. It is a renewed mind that makes possibilities happen.

"I beseech you therefore, brethren, by the mercies of God, that ye present your bodies a living sacrifice, holy, acceptable unto God, which is your reasonable service. And be not conformed to this world: but be ye transformed by the renewing of your mind, that ye may prove what is that good, and acceptable, and perfect, will of God." (Romans 12:1-2, KJV)

The degree to which your mind is renewed is the same degree to which your mind is opened to divine inspiration and divine insights.

A possibility is the state of being possible. If you have a goal that you want to achieve and if you can conceive it in your mind and think about it, then that goal is possible. Someone thought of creating a chair, and that led to a series of things that brought the chair into creation. Someone thought it would be possible to create something that blows air current around us so that we would feel cooler when it is hot, and they came up with a fan.

If you think that you can make it, that it is possible for you to be a success, to move forward in life, then you are on the right path for actualization.

Prosperity starts with the word of God in our mind, in our soul. It starts with our ability to conceive ideas. If you think you cannot make it, you cannot be promoted, you cannot move forward. If you think you cannot do business or you cannot prosper, then you will not be able to move forward. But, if you accept that whatever you want to be or do is possible, then you have opened the door up for possibilities. Whatever you can think of can be done, can exist, can happen.

Let us read Gen 11:1-8.

"And the whole earth was of one language, and of one speech. And it came to pass, as they journeyed from the east, that they found a plain in the land of Shinar; and they dwelt there. And they said one to another, Go to, let us make brick, and burn them throughly. And they had brick for stone, and slime had they for morter. And they said, Go to, let us build us a city and a tower, whose top may reach unto heaven; and let us make us a name, lest we be scattered abroad upon the face of the whole earth. And the LORD came down to see the city and the tower, which the children of men builded. And the LORD said, Behold, the people is one, and they have all one language; and this they begin to do: and now nothing will be restrained from them, which they have imagined to do. Go to, let us go down, and there confound their language, that they may not understand one another's speech. So the LORD scattered them abroad from thence upon the face of all the earth: and they left off to build the city." (Genesis 11:1-8, KJV)

The people gathered to build a city and a tower whose top will reach the sky. They thought of it. Some of them gathered and said to each other, we should be able to build a tower. After conceiving the idea, the next questions were what do we do and how do we go about it? Some people must have gathered and

SECURING YOUR FUTURE

said we can do this; we can do that or this. They did not stop by just talking, they consulted, they took actions, they faced difficulties, but they continued, and they saw progress. God also saw the progress and He said, "If I don't do something these people will get somewhere."

If you apply that to yourself, if you have an idea, talk to somebody. If that person does not catch the idea, go to somebody else. You will eventually get someone to work with you in turning your idea to reality.

The church auditorium now looks incredibly beautiful. But it has not always been like that. I asked at a time, would it be possible to have a church auditorium that is air-conditioned, what do I do? I asked questions. Somebody linked me up with an architect. The architect came to the church auditorium, looked around and said we cannot build up so as not to disobey the government's directive, but we can use glass. I asked him to draw up a design. He came up with a design that displayed the different kinds of ceilings that we could use. We needed resources to execute the project. Right in our midst, we found people that could do most of the things required for the project. We did not have to go too far to put it up. But everything started with an idea. We consulted, checked, and verified before going ahead with the plan. That was exactly what those people did in Genesis 11. But, if you start with an idea and it remains in your mind and you do not do anything about it, till next year, it will remain there.

The Bible tells us in 1 Samuel 17 about David who brought food for his brothers and heard Goliath boasting.

"And David left his carriage in the hand of the keeper of the carriage, and ran into the army, and came and saluted his brethren. And as he talked with them, behold, there came up the champion, the Philistine of Gath, Goliath by name, out of the armies of the Philistines, and spake according to the same words: and David

90

HARNESSING THE POSSIBILITIES OF THE MIND

heard them. And all the men of Israel, when they saw the man, fled from him, and were sore afraid. And the men of Israel said, Have ye seen this man that is come up? surely to defy Israel is he come up: and it shall be, that the man who killeth him, the king will enrich him with great riches, and will give him his daughter, and make his father's house free in Israel. And David spake to the men that stood by him, saying, What shall be done to the man that killeth this Philistine, and taketh away the reproach from Israel? for who is this uncircumcised Philistine, that he should defy the armies of the living God? And the people answered him after this manner, saying, So shall it be done to the man that killeth him. And Eliab his eldest brother heard when he spake unto the men; and Eliab's anger was kindled against David, and he said, Why camest thou down hither? and with whom hast thou left those few sheep in the wilderness? I know thy pride, and the naughtiness of thine heart; for thou art come down that thou mightest see the battle. And David said, What have I now done? Is there not a cause? And he turned from him toward another, and spake after the same manner: and the people answered him again after the former manner. And when the words were heard which David spake, they rehearsed them before Saul: and he sent for him. And David said to Saul, Let no man's heart fail because of him; thy servant will go and fight with this Philistine." (1 Samuel 17:22-32, KJV)

David must have seen and heard Goliath shouting. He saw the Israelite soldiers running and quaking with fear. He may have been afraid but in his heart, he said, "With God on my side, I can deal with this man." He went to ask someone, "What will happen if I deal with this man?" The person told him, so David consulted with somebody else and then another person till he got a similar answer.

Before David started consulting, what did he have in his mind? In his mind was the possibility that he could deal with the giant. When Saul said to him, "You are a small boy, how do you want to do it?" He said, "The God that delivered me from the paw of the

SECURING YOUR FUTURE

lion and delivered me from the paw of the bear, he will deliver me from this uncircumcised Philistine."

It started with the mind, not money, not strength, not weapons. It started with the mind. It always starts with the mind and then the consultation comes in. David asked questions and he got answers. He was told that he would get the king's daughter in marriage if he defeated Goliath, so his idea became even more attractive. He now had a good reason to do it. There was a goal and there was an attraction. There was something in it for him. David agreed to the proposition. Goliath came, made some noise, but David's confidence was in God. His confidence was that with his ability in God, he would defeat the giant. And he did it. But it all started with the mind. It continued with consultation and was strengthened by what he hoped to get as a result.

We also see this same principle displayed in the life of Samson after his eyes had been plucked out in Judges 16: 25-30.

"And it came to pass, when their hearts were merry, that they said, Call for Samson, that he may make us sport. And they called for Samson out of the prison house; and he made them sport: and they set him between the pillars. And Samson said unto the lad that held him by the hand, Suffer me that I may feel the pillars whereupon the house standeth, that I may lean upon them. Now the house was full of men and women; and all the lords of the Philistines were there; and there were upon the roof about three thousand men and women, that beheld while Samson made sport. And Samson called unto the LORD, and said, O Lord GOD, remember me, I pray thee, and strengthen me, I pray thee, only this once, O God, that I may be at once avenged of the Philistines for my two eyes. And Samson took hold of the two middle pillars upon which the house stood, and on which it was borne up, of the one with his right hand, and of the other with his left. And Samson said, Let me die with the Philistines. And he bowed himself with all his might; and the house fell upon the lords, and upon all the people that were therein. So the dead which he slew at

his death were more than they which he slew in his life." (Judges 16:25-30, KJV)

The Philistines said, "Bring Samson out, we want to make a sport of him." All the Philistines excited. As he came out, he thought of the possibility of dealing with these people. His eyes had been removed, so he was blind. Samson consulted by asking a small boy, "Where are the pillars?"

After you have accepted the possibility, do not attempt to do everything by yourself, if you need to ask questions, ask questions. If you need help from somebody, ask for help. Samson asked, "Small boy, where are the pillars of this place? Put my hands on the pillars." At the end of the day, the boy also died because he did not know what was about to happen. Samson also died because he chose to die as well. But you do not have to die or cause the death of those who help you along the way. The point I want to bring out is that it started with an idea.

We have gone over three examples: the tower that came from the power of imagination, David and Goliath, and Samson and the Philistines. It all started with the mind, why do you think yours would be different? That goal that you have of becoming a success is going to start with your mind. If it does not start with the mind, you have not started your journey. Once you have the possibility or idea in your mind, then it can happen. But it does not stop with the idea, you must consult, talk to someone you can get help from, and then act.

Everything in life starts as a thought, hope, or dream in somebody's mind. Do you know some people are planning to take a vacation on the moon? Do you know where it started? Somebody thought about it. People have already gone to the moon more than once. Then, somebody thought can we go for a holiday on the moon? Just as people go to America for holiday, let us go to the moon.

Then they would have thought about it a little more and discussed the idea with other people to see whether it was feasible or possible. If the response is positive, they would begin to make further enquiries and research to find out what would be needed to make the idea a reality. With more information and consultation, the idea grows to become a project that can be executed.

When you set goals, it unlocks your mind which releases ideas and the energy to pursue it. That is the reason you should set goals such as "I want to become this or become that." The mind is locked but if you can unlock it by setting goals, you will be surprised at the possibilities that it would release in the form of ideas, and that is what will energise you to start consulting, planning, and acting.

Prayer

Father I declare I can do all things through Christ which strengthens me. I receive illumination, inspiration, and innovative ideas to act upon, so that new things can begin to emerge all around me in Jesus' name. Amen.

Chapter Ten

Dealing With The Limitations In Your Mind

Once you have difficulties in your thinking, you limit your potential, you limit your abilities, and you begin to think the possibilities that come into your mind are impossible to accomplish. You begin to dwell on the impossibilities. The Bible states in Proverbs 22:13,

"The slothful man saith, There is a lion without, I shall be slain in the streets." (Proverbs 22:13, KJV)

In the mind of the lazy man, there is a possibility that there is a lion outside. He tells himself, "There is no way I can go out." He stays at home because he is thinking that there is a possibility that a lion is outside. He dwells on the thought or feeling that he cannot make it, that he is not worthy enough. If you entertain such thoughts, you are limiting yourself. Pray that every limitation will be destroyed in Jesus' name. Amen.

The Bible says as a man thinketh in his heart so is he. If you can think as the Bible says in Philippians 4:13, it will be the force that is operating in your mind and it will make you take steps that will move you forward.

"I can do all things through Christ which strengtheneth me."
(Philippians 4:13, KJV)

If you allow discouragement to settle in, as a result of the things happening around you, it will limit your potential, so you must deal with discouragement when it comes.

Something happened to me some time ago, I had received one of the results from my Masters' program. I passed, but not as much as I wanted so I felt slightly discouraged. There is a demon called discouragement that brings people down when it is allowed to settle in the mind. The Lord laid it on my mind to spend the night praying and re-affirming to myself that I will not be a failure, that I will not be discouraged, that the Bible says I am the head, that I can make it, and that I can do all things through Christ that strengthens me. I spent a lot of time praying about the things which I refused to be and declaring the things which I desired to be. The discouraging feeling was lifted because I chose to affirm the Word of God concerning my life.

In Jeremiah 1:4-10,

"Then the word of the LORD came unto me, saying, Before I formed thee in the belly I knew thee; and before thou camest forth out of the womb I sanctified thee, and I ordained thee a prophet unto the nations. Then said I, Ah, Lord GOD! behold, I cannot speak: for I am a child. But the LORD said unto me, Say not, I am a child: for thou shalt go to all that I shall send thee, and whatsoever I command thee thou shalt speak. Be not afraid of their faces: for I am with thee to deliver thee, saith the LORD. Then the LORD put forth his hand, and touched my mouth. And the LORD said unto me, Behold, I have put my words in thy mouth. See, I have this day set thee over the nations and over the kingdoms, to root out, and to pull down, and to destroy, and to throw down, to build, and to plant." (Jeremiah 1:4-10, KJV)

DEALING WITH THE LIMITATIONS IN YOUR MIND

God had a plan for Jeremiah's life. The same God that had a plan for Jeremiah has the same plan for you and I. Even while in the womb God ordained him to be a prophet. He has ordained you to be somebody even from the womb. He shared that with Jeremiah, and he wanted Jeremiah to do some things. But Jeremiah said, "I am but a child." In his own mind he was limiting himself. Jeremiah was behaving like the man who says that there is a lion outside. He said I cannot do what you want me to do because I am a child, but God said I know you are a child, but He told him not to be afraid. He told him what He has given him. He said, "I have put my words in your mind, I have deposited some things in you." He told him he has set him over nations and kingdoms to do this and this and that.

In the same way, God is saying, "I have a plan for you, my thoughts towards you are thoughts of peace and not of evil, to give you an expected end." He has a plan for you. There are certain things that He wants you to do. He has deposited treasures in your life and placed people around you. Start having a possibility mindset. Do not have the mindset that tells you that you cannot do it because of one limitation or the other, whether it's a lack of education, your finances, your background, or that you cannot understand the required language. If you have such a mindset it will limit and hinder you.

What you should be saying is that what do I need to do to overcome this hindrance? The person who designed the chair must have asked what do I need to do? That means that there is always a hindrance, limitation, or obstacle to every great pursuit, but you must find out what you need to do to overcome it. Ask yourself, "Am I to go to school? Am I to attend night classes, am I going to consult with my sister or brother or with somebody else? What do I need to learn? Maybe you would need to go to school for two years before you come back to act on the goal you have set.

When you write down your goals, write under them the things you need to do to make them possible.

Let us take time to pray for our lives, for our future according to Jeremiah 1: 4-12. Take time to pray because the foundation of your future must be laid and then there are questions you should answer.

Talk to God and pour your heart unto Him. Thank Him for your success in advance. Remember, there are people who have reached the top despite the obstacles and challenges in their way.

E.W Kenyon says, "*Obstacles stand in the way of the man who climbs. I don't know why this is, but I know it is true. These obstacles have to be overcome but in the overcoming one fits himself for places of responsibility. I thank God for poverty, for need of self-denial, for self-culture, for long hours of study and hard work. The inward drive to to plod on when tired is the thing which makes men strong, self reliant conquerors. Every failure stimulates them to harder work. There is no giving up. There is no yielding.*

Facing impossible circumstances should become a daily experience to the conqueror. He knows to trust in the Lord with all his heart and not to lean on his own understanding. He learns to win, he has cultivated the will to win, the will to conquer. He kept the fires of ambition burning, he has made work a part of himself. He has a group of very fine habits. He has the habit of study, the habit of control of his eyes and ears, the control of his passions and ambitions. He is master. He is the man who uses the public library and second-hand bookstores. He is ever studying to improve himself in his place. He knows his trade, his business, his profession, He makes himself an authority in his particular field. He counts his handicaps a blessing. He goes on with God and wins. No man is a failure until he lies down, and the undertaker puts him under the soil." (Kenyon 1966, Page 51-52),

---

Prayer

Father I declare I am not a failure. I know that I am fearfully and wonderfully made. I will not be stagnant. I will not be limited. I am determined to move forward and overcome in Jesus' name. Amen.

Chapter Eleven

Mapping Out Plans Of Action

It is what you draw from the verses of Scripture that you read or hear that becomes a revelation to you. Then you take it to the place of prayer and pray on it.

The General Overseer of RCCG once said during a ministration that as a believer, your miracle or solution is nearer than when you think. But, our eyes and hearts are often closed. The solution is in the deposits that God has placed in your life or the resources He has placed around you.

What are you doing with the deposits of God in your life or the resources He has placed around you? What you do with these deposits reflects the kind of person you are. As your mind opens to possibilities, then you need to act.

Generally, there are four types of people depending on how you use the deposits that the Lord has placed in and around you.

1. A Drifter

A drifter is someone who makes no effort to discover the deposits of God in his life. He has no dream and he only has a vague hope. He does not have any specific goals nor a plan nor a timetable that will assist in setting him on the path God has ordained him to go. Matthew 25:24-30 says,

"Then he which had received the one talent came and said, Lord, I knew thee that thou art an hard man, reaping where thou hast not sown, and gathering where thou hast not strawed: And I was afraid, and went and hid thy talent in the earth: lo, there thou hast that is thine. His lord answered and said unto him, Thou wicked and slothful servant, thou knewest that I reap where I sowed not, and gather where I have not strawed: Thou oughtest therefore to have put my money to the exchangers, and then at my coming I should have received mine own with usury. Take therefore the talent from him, and give it unto him which hath ten talents. For unto every one that hath shall be given, and he shall have abundance: but from him that hath not shall be taken away even that which he hath. And cast ye the unprofitable servant into outer darkness: there shall be weeping and gnashing of teeth." (Matthew 25:24-30, KJV)

A good example is the servant who went to bury the talents that his master gave him because he had no sense of direction. His decisions for his life are based on other people's decisions for his own life as he is easily swayed from one thing to another. If your life is filled with other people telling you what to do before you act, you are a drifter.

I am not saying it is wrong to seek other people's advice or help, but your life should not depend completely on what others can do for you. You should learn to pray to God, study the Word, and seek God's direction for your life. Do not expect your Pastor to do all the praying for you. Your Pastor may be praying for you, but he cannot be more concerned about your problem than you are. If your brother or friend or anybody helps you in life, it is because God has enabled him to help you. If anyone you have been looking up to disappoints you, you should not become shattered. It is easy for man to disappoint. But when you know that your life is in God's hands, and that

MAPPING OUT PLANS OF ACTION

it is through Him that you can move forward in life, then you will not be a drifter.

"A man's heart deviseth his way: but the LORD directeth his steps." (Proverbs 16:9, KJV)

Do not be a drifter. Make your own decisions as directed by God.

2. The Pursuer

A pursuer is someone who recognises that he has deposits of God in his life and has a dream of a good life, but he has no definite plan of how to achieve it. He is motivated by what he sees or can get, but he is short-term focused and depends more on himself than on being led by God.

A good example is the prodigal son in Luke 15: 11-14.

"And he said, A certain man had two sons: And the younger of them said to his father, Father, give me the portion of goods that falleth to me. And he divided unto them his living. And not many days after the younger son gathered all together, and took his journey into a far country, and there wasted his substance with riotous living. And when he had spent all, there arose a mighty famine in that land; and he began to be in want." (Luke 15:11-14, KJV)

Another example is Lot, the nephew of Abraham, in Gen 13: 8-11.

"And Abram said unto Lot, Let there be no strife, I pray thee, between me and thee, and between my herdmen and thy herdmen; for we be brethren. Is not the whole land before thee? separate thyself, I pray thee, from me: if thou wilt take the left hand, then I will go to the right; or if thou depart to the right hand, then I will go to the left. And Lot lifted up his eyes, and beheld all the plain of Jordan, that it was well watered

everywhere, before the LORD destroyed Sodom and Gomorrah, even as the garden of the LORD, like the land of Egypt, as thou comest unto Zoar. Then Lot chose him all the plain of Jordan; and Lot journeyed east: and they separated themselves the one from the other." (Genesis 13:8-11, KJV)

They both despised the formal authority placed above them and took decisions based on their limited vision and feelings. The prodigal son wanted to enjoy life, so he went to his father and said, "Give me my own portion." He asked for his inheritance even while his father was still alive because he was impatient. A pursuer cannot delay gratification. He wants something and he wants it immediately, even before he is prepared to handle it. The young man went and spent all his inheritance. He did not have a plan or goal. He did not invest any part of it. Everything was spent on worthless things.

Lot is another example of a pursuer. Abraham and Lot did not have any problems between themselves. The quarrel was between the servants of Abraham and the servants of Lot. Abraham told Lot, "We can't continue like this. You are a big man now. I am a big man. Let us separate. Wherever you go, I go the other way."

Lot was Abraham's nephew and he ought to have said, "Uncle, you choose first. After you choose, I'll choose." But Lot looked around and saw the area that looked pleasurable with good pasture. He did not know that not all that glitters is gold.

Do you want to change your job to another one that seems to be good or are you interested in getting involved in a business that supposedly yields high returns? Before you take such an action, make sure that God is giving you the go-ahead to take up the job or to do the business. Lot went, but the place turned out to be full of so much sin that God had to destroy the land.

He and his family had to leave without a single thing. He was a pursuer. A pursuer loves the good life, but does not have a plan, and does not seek God's counsel before making major life decisions. A drifter would not take any action except he is propelled by other people. A pursuer is ever ready to act, but without God's counsel. Do not be a pursuer. Acknowledge the Lord in all your ways and receive specific direction for your life. Prayerfully begin to set goals and receive grace towards the accomplishment of your God-given dreams.

3. The Achiever

The Achiever has discovered and can deploy the deposits of God in his life. He has a dream of a better tomorrow and he has prayerfully set out personal goals for himself. His focus, however, is only on himself and he does not have any goals to impact his family, neighbourhood, nation, or generations after him. A good example is Jabez whose mother had borne him in sorrow.

"And Jabez was more honourable than his brethren: and his mother called his name Jabez, saying, Because I bare him with sorrow. And Jabez called on the God of Israel, saying, Oh that thou wouldest bless me indeed, and enlarge my coast, and that thine hand might be with me, and that thou wouldest keep me from evil, that it may not grieve me! And God granted him that which he requested." (1 Chronicles 4:9-10, KJV)

He asked God to bless him indeed, and enlarge his coast, that God's hand would be with him and that God would keep him from evil so that he would not have pain. He was noticeably clear in his prayer point to God because he had specific goals and God granted him his request.

4. The Super Achiever

An example of a Super Achiever is David. He had a dream of a better tomorrow and he had well laid out plans that he received from God. The plan was not focused on himself alone. It was not just about what he wanted, but about what God had laid in his heart. His own goals were based on what God wanted and how he could impact his community and generation positively.

"And David assembled all the princes of Israel, the princes of the tribes, and the captains of the companies that ministered to the king by course, and the captains over the thousands, and captains over the hundreds, and the stewards over all the substance and possession of the king, and of his sons, with the officers, and with the mighty men, and with all the valiant men, unto Jerusalem. Then David the king stood up upon his feet, and said, Hear me, my brethren, and my people: As for me, I had in mine heart to build an house of rest for the ark of the covenant of the LORD, and for the footstool of our God, and had made ready for the building: But God said unto me, Thou shalt not build an house for my name, because thou hast been a man of war, and hast shed blood. Howbeit the LORD God of Israel chose me before all the house of my father to be king over Israel for ever: for he hath chosen Judah to be the ruler; and of the house of Judah, the house of my father; and among the sons of my father he liked me to make me king over all Israel: And of all my sons, (for the LORD hath given me many sons,) he hath chosen Solomon my son to sit upon the throne of the kingdom of the LORD over Israel. And he said unto me, Solomon thy son, he shall build my house and my courts: for I have chosen him to be my son, and I will be his father." (1 Chronicles 28:1-6)

In this account, David wanted to build a house for God. But God said, "You cannot build for me, your hand is filled with blood. But your son is going to build it." God told him where He wanted the house to be built, what He wanted, and how He wanted the house to be built. God had given him a plan and specific guidelines.

"Furthermore David the king said unto all the congregation, Solomon my son, whom alone God hath chosen, is yet young and tender, and the work is great: for the palace is not for man, but for the LORD God. Now I have prepared with all my might for the house of my God the gold for things to be made of gold, and the silver for things of silver, and the brass for things of brass, the iron for things of iron, and wood for things of wood; onyx stones, and stones to be set, glistering stones, and of divers colours, and all manner of precious stones, and marble stones in abundance. Moreover, because I have set my affection to the house of my God, I have of mine own proper good, of gold and silver, which I have given to the house of my God, over and above all that I have prepared for the holy house, Even three thousand talents of gold, of the gold of Ophir, and seven thousand talents of refined silver, to overlay the walls of the houses withal: The gold for things of gold, and the silver for things of silver, and for all manner of work to be made by the hands of artificers. And who then is willing to consecrate his service this day unto the LORD? Then the chief of the fathers and princes of the tribes of Israel, and the captains of thousands and of hundreds, with the rulers of the king's work, offered willingly," (1 Chronicles 29:1-6, KJV)

In the above passage, David went out of his way to prepare the money and all the resources that will be required to build the house for God. David had a God ordained plan. It was not a small plan, but a big plan and it came to pass. May the plans of God for your life also come to pass.

Apostle Paul is also another clear example of a super achiever who went out of his way to accomplish great things for the gospel.

The question now is, "What kind of plans do you have for your life? Is it a plan for tomorrow? Good. Is it a plan for next month? Good. Is it a plan for the next five, ten years? What kind of plan do you have?"

Will the plan impact your community and generation? Remember, whatever plan you have, take it back to God. Those plans could come from the place of prayer so that you will know that it is not your plan, but that God gave it to you.

You should ask the question, "Lord what would you have me do? What are the things ahead for me? What steps do you want me to take?" If you take an action that God specifically asks you to take, you will get outstanding results. If Moses threw the rod on the ground just because he wanted to, nothing would have happened, but a miracle happened because God told him to throw it. If the widow of Elisha's servant had poured oil into vessels out of her own volition, nothing would have happened. Something happened because she followed a divine instruction. The Bible gives us some guidelines in Habakkuk 2: 1-4.

"I will stand upon my watch, and set me upon the tower, and will watch to see what he will say unto me, and what I shall answer when I am reproved. And the LORD answered me, and said, Write the vision, and make it plain upon tables, that he may run that readeth it. For the vision is yet for an appointed time, but at the end it shall speak, and not lie: though it tarry, wait for it; because it will surely come, it will not tarry. Behold, his soul which is lifted up is not upright in him: but the just shall live by his faith." (Habakkuk 2:1-4, KJV)

To get a bearing on the direction to take, you need to go to the Lord and stand before Him in the place of prayer to receive specific visions and instructions. Do not relent until you receive something tangible from the Lord, which gives you an idea of what the future holds. Even if it appears that there is a delay, hold on by faith in the place of prayer until the vision comes to pass.

When you receive the plan, break it down into actionable goals for the day, week, and month. Put a system in place to review and measure how much progress you are making. If there are obstacles along the way, go back to the Lord in prayer and receive wisdom and direction on what to do. Pay attention to the leading of the Holy Spirit. He will guide you; He will teach you, and He will instruct you in the way to go.

Prayer

Father I receive inspiration to follow your plan for my life until I become a super achiever in Jesus' name. Amen.

Chapter Twelve

Receiving Answers From God

Faith is required in order to receive from God. The Bible says in Hebrews 11:6,

"But without faith it is impossible to please him: for he that cometh to God must believe that he is, and that he is a rewarder of them that diligently seek him." (Hebrews 11:6, KJV)

First of all, when you find yourself in any situation requiring direction, go to Him in the place of prayer, worship Him, and ask Him for directions. Tell Him to guide you by His Word as laid out in the Bible. If He gives you a word then run with the word. By faith ask God, "What would you have me do with this word?" He may give you a set of instructions to follow. He may not give you. If He does not give you, wait on Him until you have something tangible or specific that you can work with. I pray that God will open your eyes for revelation, direction, insights, and understanding.

2 Corinthians 4:4 says,

"In whom the god of this world hath blinded the minds of them which believe not, lest the light of the glorious gospel of

Christ, who is the image of God, should shine unto them." (2 Corinthians 4:4, KJV)

It is possible for your mind to be blinded, but through prayer whatever has blinded your eyes will be removed in Jesus' name. In Jeremiah 1:11-14 the Bible says,

"Moreover the word of the LORD came unto me, saying, Jeremiah, what seest thou? And I said, I see a rod of an almond tree. Then said the LORD unto me, Thou hast well seen: for I will hasten my word to perform it. And the word of the LORD came unto me the second time, saying, What seest thou? And I said, I see a seething pot; and the face thereof is toward the north. Then the LORD said unto me, Out of the north an evil shall break forth upon all the inhabitants of the land." (Jeremiah 1:11-14, KJV)

God was asking, 'What do you see?' And he responded, 'I see this'. And God made him to understand that He will hasten His word to perform it.

The first prayer point is that there is a need to pray for God to open your eyes to see the opportunity, the potential, and the possibility.

Secondly, there is a need for prayer in order to know what to do. The Bible says in James 1:5,

"If any of you lack wisdom, let him ask of God, that giveth to all men liberally, and upbraideth not; and it shall be given him." (James 1:5, KJV)

I have learnt to pray that prayer a lot. Holy Spirit, what would You have me do now? How do I go about it? What do I do now?

For instance, I went back to graduate school to pursue a Masters' degree in Logistics and Supply Chain Management in Cranfield, United Kingdom. Most of the time, between 1 a.m. and 4 a.m., I would be awake, reading. What would make a man at my age return to school? I believed that there were things in me that I had to develop. As a person, there are five things that I am trusting God for in my life: I want to be a homemaker, I want to fulfil ministry, I want to be a Christian business leader, I want to be a financial pillar, and I want to be a relationship builder. I did not just decide I wanted these things. I spent time in the place of prayer. I prayed, "Lord help me to be a homemaker, to fulfil the ministry you have given me, to be a business leader, and to be a financial pillar."

I asked myself "With this job that I am doing today, can I become a financial pillar?" I can sow the resources I get from the job, but will that enable me to attain the level I want to attain? What do I need to do? I realised that I could go back to school and obtain more knowledge. I went back to God. He gave me a leading and I followed it. Before I completed the course, I asked Him, "I shall soon finish this course, what next? What lies ahead? What opportunities are waiting for me?" I did not get a specific answer, but I had an assurance within me that all will be well. I knew that He will prepare me for whatever lies ahead.

Ten years have passed since I obtained my master's degree and when I look back, I am very thankful to the Lord for blessing me, for enlarging my coast, and for opening up well placed executive roles for me.

The Lord will give you whatever you need for your tomorrow. The provision is already there, even the one you need for today.

Thirdly, having developed yourself you need to prayerfully identify the assets and the resources that God has placed around you that will lead you to solve challenges or become a solution provider.

When our church had the challenge with the use of our auditorium, the people God used to solve the problem were people we have always known. We always had them around us. God just used that particular situation and connected the lines together. Solutions are manifested when the lines around us are connected.

Fourthly, pray for strength to bring forth. It is possible to get pregnant, and then struggle to bring forth. You may be pregnant with an idea, or a vision, and you are struggling to bring it forth. Pray for strength to bring forth the idea that has been conceived.

Fifthly, take a step of faith. Having prayed and prayed, having asked for wisdom, having asked for strength and God has laid something in your heart, take a step of faith. As you take that step, if something comes up like a red light in your spirit and you can perceive in your heart that you should not go, do not go! If, however you perceive a green light, saying 'Go' in your spirit, then, go ahead. Take a step of faith. Many of us have prayed, but the step of faith that we need to take is where many of us are lacking. Once you take that step, the Bible says, in all your ways acknowledge Him and He shall direct thy path. The Bible says the Holy One of Israel will teach you to profit and lead you in the way to go.

E.W. Kenyon says, "*You are standing on the threshold. Before you lie the untried paths. What are you going to do? Have you chosen your work, your vocation ,your place in life or are you drifting, hoping that something will turn up? It will but, the thing that turns up may be of no value to you unless you are ready to take it as it comes. Don't float. Dead fish float. Make up your mind that you will put your dreams into blue prints and then with the blue prints in your hand, you will build your mansion. Find your place, but be sure that you do thorough preparatory work. Put real hard work into the days of preparation. Don't just get by. Don't be satisfied with anything but one hundred plus. Fight for it. Work for it. Enjoy it. Make it a game to win. Be a success in youth and you will be a success in middle life. You will be crowned in old age. Make yourself a wanted person. Be so valuable that if you have to move, men and women would weep because of your departure. If you plan to be a minister, be God's best. If you go into business, be the best in your community. If you plan to be a lawyer or a physician, put a trained, cultured personality into it. Whatever you do, plan to build your house on top of the hill. Harness that lazy mind and make it work. That mind can make a place for you. Let me say again unto you, "Go under your own steam". Prepare yourself and doors will open to you everywhere."* (Kenyon 1966, Page 69-70)

As we conclude this book, the following are some particularly important questions that you need to prayerfully ask yourself and answer about your personal life. If you answer the questions below sincerely, they will give you an insight into the plan of God for your life so that you can take the corresponding steps to actualising the plan of God for your life.

1. What are the plans and purposes of God for your life?

Do you know the Lord has good plans for you? He wants you to excel, to be fruitful, to multiply, to live an abundant life, to be a blessing to your generation, and to reach Heaven.

Pray that God will reveal His plan for your life.

2. What has God deposited inside of you?

The Lord has already placed in your life all that you need to be a success: talents, potential, gifts, ideas, abilities, skills, and creativity.

You need to identify the ones that you have. These are the things that make you what you are. It is what you have in you that counts. If you are yet to do something about them, they are still undeveloped resources and untouched treasures that are stored inside of you. Potential is simply an innate ability that

SECURING YOUR FUTURE

has not yet been tapped. It cannot be seen, but is able to do great things. The potential of an average person is like a huge ocean unsailed, a new continent unexplored, a world of possibilities waiting to be released and channelled toward some great good.

Pray that God will open your eyes and your heart to see, know, and understand the use of the things He has placed in your life.

3. What resources has God placed around you? The Lord has promised that He will never leave us nor forsake us. All around us He has strategically placed People, the Word, Assets, and Opportunities. It is only when we open our eyes, or He opens our eyes, that we realise what He has placed around us.

Pray that God will open your eyes and your heart to see, know and appreciate the various assets He has placed around you so that you can begin to utilise them effectively.

4. What does God want you to do with His deposits in your life?

He wants you to develop them. Do not be like the servant in the parable of the talents who went to hide the deposits that had been given to him. Every God given deposit in your life has been given for a specific purpose in the grand master plan of God for your life.

Pray for the Lord to open your eyes, for revelation, for illumination, for direction, for insights, for understanding to know His plan and purpose for placing these deposits in and around your life.

5. What must you do to live a pain free, peaceful, prosperous, and purposeful life?

Everyone wants to be a success, live in good health without strife or confusion, and be able to meet their basic needs.

Pray that the Lord will cause your life to be pain free, peaceful, prosperous, and purposeful.

6. How can you be a blessing to your generation?

Super achievers are not just thinking about themselves; they are also thinking about being a blessing to others. Being able to help others and having enough to give to them makes you a blessing in the lives of other people"

Pray that you will be a blessing and a source of joy to your generation.

7. What legacy does God want you to leave behind when it is time to go home?

Everyone has what it takes to be a blessing, to leave an inheritance for their children's children, to make a significant mark in their community, and to leave a legacy behind.

Pray that your legacy will be a witness to many generations.

Last Words And Prayers

If you really want to secure your future, develop a habit of always thanking God for all that He is doing in your life. Do not murmur or complain. The Israelites that murmured in the wilderness on their way to the Promised Land were all destroyed. Complaining can destroy your future. But, when you have an attitude of appreciation and thanksgiving for the little you have, God will release more to you. Learn to say thank you to God and He will give you more. Pray fervently. Prayer is an investment for your future. The Bible says in James 5:16 that the effectual fervent prayer of a righteous man bringeth much. Prayers determine what will happen ahead. If you are not spending quality time praying and thanking God, then you are leaving your future hanging without a base. May your life not be like that in the name of Jesus.

You can start today to position yourself for change. You can choose to align with the Master, the one who knows the end from the beginning. You can choose to obey His Word. Identify which area of your life is insecure, your finances, your marriage, your career, your children then apply God's word to secure it.

Jesus was speaking in John 14:1-3.

"Let not your heart be troubled: ye believe in God, believe also in me. In my Father's house are many mansions: if it were not so, I would have told you. I go to prepare a place for you. And if

I go and prepare a place for you, I will come again, and receive you unto myself; that where I am, there ye may be also." (John 14:1-3, KJV)

Jesus has gone to prepare and secure a future place for us in heaven. Are you living your life such that you will get to heaven? The Bible says in 1 Timothy 4:8,

"For bodily exercise profiteth little: but godliness is profitable unto all things, having promise of the life that now is, and of that which is to come." (1 Timothy 4:8, KJV)

Godliness is profitable for the life that now is and the life which is to come.

Will you allow the place that Jesus has prepared for you to be vacant? Your character and lifestyle will determine whether you get to inherit your heavenly home.

If you have not yet accepted Jesus as your Lord and personal saviour, right now is a golden opportunity to do so. You may just have been a professing Christian, without a right relationship. Today, you can make amends. You can have a new beginning that will change your life and secure a glorious future for you.

By making this decision, you will ensure that the place He has reserved for you in Heaven will not be vacant. All you need to do is to accept Jesus as your Lord and personal Saviour and to confess with your mouth that Jesus is Lord in your life.

"That if thou shalt confess with thy mouth the Lord Jesus, and shalt believe in thine heart that God hath raised him from the dead, thou shalt be saved. For with the heart man believeth unto righteousness; and with the mouth confession is made unto salvation." (Romans 10:9-10, KJV)

Pray like this:

Lord Jesus, I confess my sins and I ask that you please forgive me. I believe you died for me to receive eternal life so please come and take your place in my heart today.

If you prayed this prayer, please join a Bible believing church and begin to fellowship regularly there. As you do so, you will grow in the Lord and your future will be secured in Jesus' name.

Last Words

This book, Securing Your Future, was first written and completed in 2010. At the point of printing the book, I had a restraint in my spirit man. It was similar to what I had read in 1 Samuel 17:39 when Saul gave David his armour to use against Goliath. David said, "I have not proved them." I also felt that I needed to prove the principles and nuggets that I had shared in the book. Ten years later now, I can say with boldness and confidence that there is power in the Word of God. The Word of God is yea and amen. I have seen the Word of God come alive at the right time in several situations and it has secured for me a glorious future. God is never late. The Word of God works wonders. I therefore leave you with this scripture in Acts 20:32.

"And now, brethren, I commend you to God, and to the word of his grace, which is able to build you up, and to give you an inheritance among all them which are sanctified". (Acts 20:32 KJV)

I look forward to hearing and reading about your testimonies as you follow God's system, the Word of God, to secure your future and the future of your children's children in Christ Jesus.

God bless you richly in Jesus' name.

Oladapo Olarinmoye

References

1. Kenyon E.W. 1966. Sign Posts on the Road to Success. 16th ed. USA. Kenyon's Gospel Publishing Society.

CPSIA information can be obtained
at www.ICGtesting.com
Printed in the USA
LVHW091225171220
674414LV00005B/713